THE BABY-SITTERS CLUB

GUIDE TO BABY-SITTING

JAHNNA BEECHAM

and

MALCOLM HILLGARTNER

SCHOLASTIC INC.

New York   Toronto   London   Auckland   Sydney

Special thanks to
Dr. Mark Sorensen, M.D.
and Beth Sorensen, PA-C
for their careful evaluation
of the medical emergency and first-aid section

Cover art by Hodges Soileau
Interior illustrations by Nancy Didion
Medical emergency and first-aid procedures illustrated by Tony Talarico

ISBN 0-590-47686-6

12 11 10 9 8 7 6 5 4 3 2 1   3 4 5 6 7 8/9

Printed in the U.S.A.   40

First Scholastic printing, November 1993

CONTENTS

▪

GUIDE TO
BABY-SITTING

FOREWORD FROM ANN M. MARTIN

■

Dear Reader,

As the members of the BSC will tell you, the baby-sitter's motto ought to be: "Be prepared." Of course, it's hard to be prepared for everything. Once when I was baby-sitting, a neighbor's golden retriever ate my charge's socks. Who could be prepared for that? Still, you might as well be prepared for the more common occurrences, such as putting your charges to bed, or taking care of a sick or injured child. Boy, was Mary Anne glad she was prepared when she baby-sat for Jenny Prezzioso and discovered Jenny was running a temperature of 104°. That's where this book comes in. It will help you to be prepared for bedtime, bathtime, mealtime, and all sorts of emergencies. It will also give you tips on babies, toddlers, and older kids, and what to expect from them.

In my opinion, a really great baby-sitter is not only prepared, he or she is creative, and knows how to make sitting a fun experience for the kids. That's why Kristy came up with the idea for Kid-Kits. It's why Claudia plans art projects for her charges. So bring this book with you on your next sitting job. In it you'll find lists of activities, songs, and stories for kids of various ages. My most memorable baby-sitters were the ones who played with my sister and me. One invented a bowling game with plastic bath toys. Another brought along art supplies and helped us make holiday ornaments. I kept those things in mind when I became a sitter myself.

Now it's your turn. So be safe, be prepared, be creative...and have fun!

Ann M. Martin

MESSAGES FROM THE BSC

A good baby-sitter likes kids. Even when they are cranky and don't want to pick up their toys or take a bath or go to bed.
— Kristy

A good baby-sitter takes his or her job seriously. She arrives on time, focuses all of her attention on the children and their welfare, and makes sure she's someone a client can trust to make mature decisions.
— Mary Anne

A good baby-sitter is creative. She or he takes the time to think of fun new games to play with the children so that they will want her to come back again and again.
— Claudia
(P.S. Thanks for the help with my spelling, Mary Anne!)

A good baby-sitter keeps calm, even in an emergency, and is able to call the right people and get help when it's needed.
— Stacey

A good baby-sitter cleans up after himself or herself and the charges and makes sure the house is neat and tidy when the clients return home.
— Dawn

A good baby-sitter gives each child equal attention.
— Mallory

A GOOD BABY-SITTER STICKS TO HIS COMMITMENT TO HIS CLIENT, EVEN WHEN FRIENDS MAKE PLANS TO DO SOMETHING FUN ON THE SAME NIGHT.
— LOGAN

a good baby-sitter knows she needs time for her homework, activities, and friends and takes that into account when she schedules her jobs.
— Jessi

A good baby-sitter doesn't cancel unless she's sick or there's a family emergency. Or unless it's something really important and she knows at least a week in advance. And even then she does her best to help her client find a good replacement.
— Shannon

IF YOU THINK YOU'D MAKE A GOOD BABY-SITTER OR WOULD LIKE TO BECOME A BETTER ONE, READ ON...

PART I
BABY-SITTING

HOW TO BECOME A GOOD BABY-SITTER

■

"BE PREPARED!"

"BE PREPARED" is the Scouts' motto but it should also be the baby-sitter's motto. Remember, you are going to be taking care of small children all by yourself. You need to be able to change a baby's diapers and feed him. You need to be able to prepare a dinner or snack, give a toddler a bath, and put her to bed. If an emergency arises, you need to know whom to call and what to do until help arrives.

"How do I prepare?"

■ Take a baby-sitting course. Many are offered by your local hospital, YMCA, or community center. Ask your teacher or school nurse for information. If no baby-sitting class is offered, call your hospital and ask about infant CPR courses (CPR stands for cardiopulmonary resuscitation, and is the technique for reviving the heart and lungs).

Mrs Prezzioso asked the BSC to take an infant care course before we took care of Andrea, and we learned really valuable information like what to do if a child is choking, and how to give artificial respiration.

— Mary Anne

■ Volunteer to be a helper at a nursery or day care center.

■ Ask your parents or neighbors if you can spend time with them one afternoon as they take care of their baby.

3

- Read. There are many books in the library on child-rearing. They all have sections on what to do in case of an emergency and many offer tips on what to expect from a baby or a toddler. For starters take a look at these:

> *Dr. Spock's Baby and Child Care*
> by Benjamin Spock & Michael B. Rothenberg
> *Your Baby and Child* by Penelope Leach
> *Your Two Year Old* (and other books in the series up through age seven) by Ames & Ilg

"How old do I have to be?"

- Most kids start to think about baby-sitting between the ages of eleven and thirteen.

I got my great idea to form the Baby-sitters Club when I was twelve.

— Kristy

- If you're not old enough to stay with kids on your own, you might consider being a mother's helper.

I started by helping Mom take care of my brothers and sisters (I've got seven!). It's a great way to learn on the job and if a problem arises, your mom is there to help you solve it. Sometimes clients just need a mother's helper to be there while they're fixing dinner or working at home.

— Mallory

- Start out slowly by limiting your hours.

I'm not allowed to baby-sit at night but I can baby-sit after school and during the day on the weekends.

— Jessi

4

GETTING THE WORD OUT

"How do I let people know I'm ready to baby-sit?"

You've taken a baby-sitting course, you've volunteered to be a mother's helper, and you've read several books on the subject. In short, you're ready to begin baby-sitting but you don't know how to get the word out.

- Tell your friends who are already baby-sitting. Ask them to recommend you when they're unable to take a job.

- Talk to your parents, their friends, your neighbors, teachers, and members of your church or temple. Also talk with day care centers.

- Type up a flier and pass it to family, friends, and local businesses that you know well. Ask for permission before you post a flier in a store. Many places have bulletin boards just for that purpose.

Make sure your advertisement is eye-catching but informative. List your name, age, and hours that you are available to sit.
— Claudia

Be sure your spelling is correct and the printing is neat. Remember, this is your first impression. Make it a good one.
— Mary Anne

Here's an example of tear-off advertising:

THE BABY-SITTERS CLUB
NEED A BABY-SITTER?
SAVE TIME! CALL KL5-3231
MONDAY, WEDNESDAY, AND FRIDAY
5:30 - 6:00 PM
AND REACH SEVEN EXPERIENCED
BABY-SITTERS
AVAILABLE: WEEKENDS,
AFTER SCHOOL, EVENINGS

KL5-3231 KL5-3231 KL5-3231 KL5-3231 KL5-3231 KL5-3231 KL5-3231 KL5-3231 KL5-3231 KL5-3231

Clients also like it when you give them a card that they can tape to their refrigerator or keep in their wallet.
— *Dawn*

NEED A RESPONSIBLE, CARING BABY-SITTER?

 KELLY SMITH
555-6889

Available to sit after school and on weekends.

"WHAT SHOULD I CHARGE?"

■ Rates per hour vary from state to state and town to town. Check with your friends and find out the going rate in your area.

6

- Some sitters charge a flat rate for one child and then an additional amount (fifty cents) per extra kid. Be aware of how many children you are capable of handling. Three is a lot, even for an adult.

Because there are so many kids in my family, my parents always hire two sitters to look after them. Sometimes families will chip in together to hire a sitter. If the number of kids is too high, suggest that the parents hire two of you.

— Mallory

- Some sitters charge more per hour for sitting after midnight (time and a half).

  NOTE: If you're going to add charges for extra children and after midnight, be sure to let your client know *before* you go to the job.

GETTING THE JOB
"What do I say when a client calls?"

- Ask how many children you'll be caring for.
- Give them your rate or, if you haven't decided on one, ask what they pay.
- Ask if you'll need transportation to and from the job.
- Ask them how late they'll be. If you can't stay out past a certain time, be sure and tell your client ahead of time.

- Ask for their address and number, and be sure to leave it with your parents.

- If this is a new client, find out who recommended you. Ask if you and one of your parents can stop by before the job and meet the children.

It's nice for the client's kids to meet you ahead of time. Then you won't feel like strangers the first time you sit for them.

—Kristy

When you do meet the kids, ask them what games they like to play and what toys are their favorite. That way you can stock your Kid-Kit with something special just for them.

— Claudia

KID-KITS

"What should I take to my baby-sitting job?"

Kid-Kits were Kristy's great idea (like everything else!). She suggested we decorate boxes and fill them with toys and art supplies and take them with us when we baby-sit.

— Mary Anne

You can decorate an old shoe box or small suitcase with sequins, paint, glitter, buttons — anything you can find that can be glued on. Be creative and have fun!

— Claudia

Claudia's Kid-Kit

■ Children don't care if the toys are new. Fill your Kid-Kit with toys from around your house that you or your younger brothers and sisters are no longer using.

■ Check-out the Goodwill or Salvation Army thrift stores. Often they have really fun, but inexpensive, toys and games.

■ The items in your Kid-Kit should be age appropriate. If you're sitting for a toddler, remember: THEY PUT EVERYTHING IN THEIR MOUTHS. Make sure you bring toys that they won't choke on.

Here are some suggestions for your Kid-Kit:

    Crayons and other art supplies
    Erasable Magic Markers
    Coloring books
    Paper dolls
    Clay-Mate
    Puzzles
    Board games (Chutes & Ladders, Candy Land, Sorry!)
    Puppets (These can be made by taking an old sock and
       attaching buttons for eyes)
    Legos

Duplos
Slinky
Jacks and a ball
Deck of cards
Softball and glove
Magic tricks

Lots of books, including:
  Mr. Popper's Penguins by Richard and Florence Atwater
  Goodnight Moon by Margaret Wise Brown
  The Goops and How to Be Them by Gelett Burgess
  Green Eggs and Ham by Dr. Seuss
  Find the Duck by Stephen Cartwright
  The Borrowers by Mary Norton
  Bootsie Barker Bites by Barbara Bottner
  There's a Nightmare in My Closet by Mercer Mayer

"What else should I take to the job?"

■ This book

At the very back of the book, under the heading important numbers, be sure and list the phone numbers of:

  1) Ambulance   4) Poison Control Center
  2) Police   5) Doctor
  3) Fire Department

It's not a bad idea to include a good solid list of back up numbers of people you can call in case you have trouble and need advice or help.
—Kristy

Also, list your own work schedule.

As secretary for the BSC, I keep track of everyone's schedules in our record book. I list the days and times they have lessons or softball practice and I also pencil in the jobs for each week. It's great to know your schedule when clients want to hire you for future jobs.
— Mary Anne

■ You might consider bringing along your own first-aid kit. That way, if an emergency arises, you won't have to search for a Band-Aid or a sterile gauze pad. You'll have it with you. A simple first-aid kit would include:

> Band-Aids
> Telfa non-stick sterile pads
> Neosporin (antibacterial ointment to put on cuts and bites)
> Ipecac (to induce vomiting in case of accidental poisoning
>   when directed by a physician or the Poison Control Center)

**Okay. You've done your research,
put the word out, and stocked your Kid-Kit.
Now the phone rings. It's your first client!**

ON YOUR MARK... GET SET... BABY-SIT!

THE BABY-SITTING JOB

■

"DING-DONG! I'M HERE!"

■ **Arrive Early**

When I sit for the Barretts, I make sure I get there at least a half an hour early. That allows enough time for Mrs. Barrett to finish getting dressed, write down phone numbers, and give me instructions for dinner.

—Dawn

■ **Dress Neatly**

It shows that you consider this a real job and you care enough to look nice for it.

—Mary Anne

■ **Act Maturely**

Parents need to feel confident that they can leave for the evening and you will be able to handle whatever arises. If you giggle and act embarrassed and shy, it's hard for them to feel confident.

— Stacey

"What should I do before the parents leave?"

- for the baby-sitter
① We are at Chez Maurice
restaurant: 555-1000
② neighbor: The Smiths
555-2000
③ Physician: Dr. Dellenkamp
555-3000
④ Our home address & phone
293 Rosedale Ave.
Stoneybrook, CT
555-4000

Make sure the clients write down:

■ The number where they can be reached (the restaurant, the movie theatre, the shopping mall)

A number of a friend or neighbor that you can call in case you can't reach them

Their doctor's phone number

The phone number and address of where you are sitting

If an emergency happens, you'll need to tell the hospital or fire department where you are. Write it down on a piece of paper by the phone and you won't worry about getting so rattled that you'll forget.

— Claudia

"What questions should I ask?"

What time is bedtime?

Do the children need a bath before bed?

What is the bedtime procedure?

Do the children need to be fed dinner? If so, what?

■ Are they allergic to any food or medication?

- How do you work the microwave or oven?

- Can the kids have snacks? Watch TV? Play outside? Have friends over to visit them? Play at a neighbor's house?

- What can't the kids do?

- Do the kids have homework they need to do?

- Do the pets need any special care?

- If this is your first time, ask for a tour of the house. Find out where diapers, towels, Band-Aids, and flashlights are kept.

WHEN KIDS COME TO YOUR HOUSE

Occasionally you might baby-sit for children at your own house. If there aren't any little kids in your family, you don't have to go out and buy outlet plugs and cupboard locks, but you should know where the hazards are in your house and what you can do to prevent any potential problems.

BEWARE OF:

1) **Stairs**—little babies and toddlers could fall down them.

2) **Electrical outlets**—children like to put things into sockets. Don't let them!

3) **Cupboards with dangerous products** like household cleaners and bug sprays. Keep kids away from them.

4) **Cords**—babies could bite through them or toddlers could trip on them.

THE CHANGING OF THE GUARD
"Mommy! Don't leave me!"

Separation anxiety is probably one of the most common problems a sitter will run into. Be assured that the tears only last a few minutes. Remain calm and cheery. The more relaxed you are about the situation, the easier it will be for the parents and the child to separate.

■ Distract the children with a special toy or game from your Kid-Kit. This will help the parents make their good-byes quickly.

■ Parents can help the separation by spending a few minutes helping you start an activity like a board game or a movie or playing with dolls. Then they can casually say good-bye.

> I sometimes ask parents for a photo album. Kids love to look at pictures of themselves. If we get started looking at pictures, then the kids forget the parents are leaving.
> —Stacey

■ Go outside with the child and wave good-bye. Mention that the parents will return.

> I always call, "See you soon!" when the parents leave. That way my charge is reassured that they're coming back.
> —Mary Anne

15

- After the parents are gone, the way to get them involved in an activity is to start playing with a toy of theirs or one from your Kid-Kit. Generally they'll get curious and sit next to you. Then you can casually start talking to them.

- If the child is still upset and missing her parents, help her make a gift to give the parents when they return.

I ask the kids to draw a special picture that we put right on the front door so the parents will see it the second they come home. —Claudia

- Ask for the child's help. Tell him you're thirsty and ask where the glasses are and if they can help you find the juice. Before they know it, they're involved with you and eager to show you other things like their room and toys.

- Take a little time before you pick a baby up. Even though they may not be able to talk, they want to get to know you before you touch them. Talk to them. Pick up their toys. Eventually they will let you know (in non-verbal ways) that it's okay to hold them.

ON YOUR OWN WITH THE KIDS
"What do we do now?"

The parents have left, feeling confident that their children are in good hands. You've got the number where they can be reached on a pad next to the phone and you also have a back-up number of a neighbor. Now it's time to have fun.

It doesn't take a whole lot to entertain babies. Mostly you need to make sure that they're safe. If they're still too little to walk, be extra careful when they're sitting on couches or beds—they could fall off. If they're able to pull themselves to their feet and scoot along furniture, make sure they don't slip on magazines on the floor.

■ Babies like to lie on their stomachs and kick their legs. Spread a blanket on the floor and put on music, so they can wiggle.

■ Babies like rattles and things that jingle or make noise.

■ Babies like to be read to. Books like *Pat the Bunny* are nice because they can feel the bunny fur and look at themselves in the mirror.

All of my brothers and sisters liked to play Peek-a-Boo when they were babies. Use your hands or a book or a diaper and watch them giggle.

—Mallory

■ Be sure and keep an eye on the baby's diaper. It's not good for a baby to spend hours in the same soggy diaper. She could get diaper rash. Check it at least once an hour and be sure and change the diaper before putting the baby to bed.

TOXIC WASTE
"How do I change the (ew! ick!) diaper?"

■ Gather your supplies BEFORE you start to change the baby. You'll need:
- — a diaper
- — diaper wipes (moist towelettes)
- — diaper rash ointment, in case the baby has a rash (A & D and Desitin are good ones)

■ Lay the baby on the changing table or on a towel on the bed or floor. IMPORTANT: KEEP ONE HAND ON THE BABY AT ALL TIMES IF SHE IS ON A TABLE OR BED. Even though babies can't walk or crawl, they can roll.

■ Slip the new, clean diaper under the baby before you take the soiled diaper off. If it is a disposable diaper, the sticky tabs go at the back and fold around toward the front. Always wipe with the towelette from the front to the back so the baby doesn't get diaper rash. If there is a rash on the baby, squeeze out a tiny glop of ointment and spread it over the rash. Then seal the diaper and *ta da!* you're done.

P.S. Dump the old diaper in a diaper pail.

WHAT TO DO WITH A TODDLER
(AGE ONE TO THREE)

This age group is into everything. One second they are pulling all of the books off the shelves and the next second they are in your purse and taking apart your wallet. The youngest toddlers can entertain themselves by trying to assemble plastic food containers. As they get closer to three, toddlers like stacking blocks and dressing dolls, or playing with clay and coloring. They still are at the age that they're playing *beside* other kids but not really *with* them.

Games and songs for one-year-olds:

Ring Around the Rosie
Peek-a-Boo
Patty Cake
This Little Piggy Went to Market

Kids love to make noise. If you can find a wooden spoon or any kind of spoon and a cardboard box, they'll create their own music. But hold your ears!
— Dawn

Games for one- to three-year-olds:

Hide and Seek
Mother, May I?
Duck, Duck, Goose
Statues
Red Light, Green Light
Simon Says

IT SEEMS THAT MOST KIDS LOVE TO BUILD FORTS. ALL YOU NEED ARE A COUPLE OF BLANKETS OR SHEETS, AND SOME CHAIRS OR A TABLE. THEN YOU CAN PRETEND TO BE PIRATES, OR PETER

PAN AND WENDY, OR DAVY CROCKETT.
FOR AN EXTRA- SPECIAL TREAT, LET
THEM EAT SNACKS INSIDE THEIR FORT.
— LOGAN

Songs for one- to three-year-olds:

The Wheels on the Bus

This Old Man

Where Is Thumbkin?

The Itsy Bitsy Spider

Old MacDonald

The Hokey Pokey

I like to put on music and dance. Sometimes we pretend we're butterflies. Sometimes we tie towels or scarves around our shoulders and play super heroes flying through the air.
— Jessi

Books for this age:

For one-year-olds: Any books with animal pictures and animal sounds. They also like the *Find the Puppy* (*Duck* or *Kitty*) books by Stephen Cartwright. And board books are great!

For all toddlers:
   Go Dog Go by P. D. Eastman

We're Going on a Bear Hunt by Helen Oxenbury
The Cat in the Hat (or anything) by Dr. Seuss
Where the Wild Things Are by Maurice Sendak

(This is just a place to start. Go to the library and pick your own books. Kids like ones with fun pictures and lots of repetition.)

WHAT TO DO WITH THREE- TO SIX-YEAR-OLDS

This age group still likes to build things with blocks and play with dolls and cars but now it's even more fun because they want to play *with* you and their brothers and sisters. They like to try to read simple books but they are also getting to the age where they enjoy listening to you read more complicated stories.

Games for three- to six-year-olds:

All of the games listed for one- to three-year-olds, plus:
Board games
Puzzles
Jacks
Marbles
Dominoes
Cards: Go Fish and Old Maid

Children love to play house and school and dress-up of any kind. Sometimes all you need is a hat or a scarf or a pair of glasses.
—Kristy

Crafts:

■ Fold paper hats out of newspaper and color them.

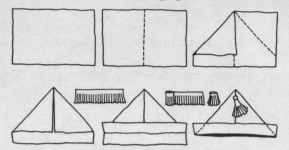

■ Make masks by cutting holes in paper bags, decorating them, and just slipping them over your head.

Books for three- to six-year-olds:

All of the books for the younger ages, plus any early readers.

> *Winnie the Pooh* by A. A. Milne
> *Babar the King* by Jean De Brunhoff
> *Rikki Tiki Tavi* by Rudyard Kipling
> *The Paper Bag Princess* by Robert Munsch
> *Clifford the Big Red Dog* by Norman Bridwell

WHAT TO DO WITH SIX-YEAR-OLDS AND UP

Once kids are in elementary school, baby-sitting is more like caring for a younger friend. They enjoy doing all of the activities previously listed and will suggest many more of their own.

When I know I'm sitting for kids in elementary school I always stock my Kid-Kit with a few more card games and board games like Risk and Monopoly.
— Stacey

Cooking projects can be lots of fun, but make sure you check with the parents first. It's better if the kids are three or over and there are no small babies around. Remember, it's awfully hard to supervise cooking and watch an infant at the same time.

—Dawn

Books for six-year-olds and up:

Charlotte's Web and *Stuart Little* by E. B. White
The Mouse and the Motorcycle (or others) by Beverly Cleary
A Bear Called Paddington by Michael Bond
James and the Giant Peach by Roald Dahl
Mary Poppins by P. L. Travers

DISCIPLINE
"Jenny hit me! WAAAAAAH!"

Sooner or later a child is going to hit you or a sister or brother, or do something that is absolutely forbidden, and you're going to have to let him know that this behavior is not acceptable. It is important to remember that you should never hit or spank the children. Ask the parents how they would like you to discipline their child.

TIME OUT

■ Time out, or some form of it, is usually used by parents. It consists of telling the children to go to another room or a special chair and sit by themselves for a few minutes. (Not a closet or a dark room. The point isn't to scare them but to allow them time to calm down.)

■ Set a timer. An easy way to determine the limit is by their age. Three-year-olds, three minutes, and so on. Explain that they need to be by themselves to calm down.

■ When the timer goes off, welcome them back, cheerily. This shows that you may not have liked their behavior, but you still like them.

"How do I get a kid to listen to me?"

Show that you respect their rights as a person. Everyone likes to know that his opinions and feelings count. No one likes being ordered around. Remember, you have been hired to be a caregiver, not a prison warden.

Respect your charges' privacy. Knock before you enter their room and let them be in the bathroom by themselves.
— Mary Anne

Offer them choices. "Would you like to pick up your toys now, or watch TV for fifteen more minutes and then pick up your toys?"

— Claudia

CHOWTIME

"I'm hungry! When are we going to eat?"

If you've been playing games and the kids are starting to get a little rambunctious, food is a great way to restore order. Make sure the children sit at a table either in the kitchen or dining room when they eat. This avoids the possibility of spills on the living room carpet. Be sure they stay in their seats until they've finished eating.

NOTE: If they sit in a high chair, make sure they're strapped in. Don't forget to loop the waist belt through the middle strap that goes between their legs. A baby can wriggle out of the waist belt and fall or get caught halfway between the chair and the floor.

LUNCH OR DINNER

The parents should have left instructions on what to feed the children for dinner. If they didn't, and you don't feel like you can cook AND keep an eye on the baby and the two-year-old, then there's nothing better than a good old-fashioned PBJ (peanut butter and jelly sandwich). Here are a few more suggestions for meals that are quick and easy:

Soup and Sandwich: Any can of soup from the cupboard and:
  ham and cheese sandwich
  turkey sandwich
  bologna sandwich
  tuna sandwich
  hot dog
  cream cheese and sunflower seed or cucumber slice sandwich

Macaroni and Cheese: This requires cooking the noodles on the stove or microwaving a frozen dish. Applesauce makes a good side dish.

Cheese Quesadillas: All you need is two flour tortillas and any kind of cheese. Make a cheese sandwich with the tortillas, then microwave it just long enough to melt the cheese (thirty seconds) or put it in the oven. Then cut the tortilla in pie wedges, and serve. This goes well with apple slices, salads, or a side of beans.

FEEDING THE BABY

■ If a baby is still drinking a bottle and on formula, check with the parents for preparation instructions. Formulas come either as a ready-to-use liquid or as a powder that needs to be mixed with water.

■ Ask your client to tell you if the bottle needs to be heated and how you should do it. Some hold the bottle under hot running water. Some fill a container with hot tap water and set the bottle in it. And although it's not generally recommended, others remove the top of the bottle and microwave the milk for thirty seconds.

NOTE: Always test the temperature of heated milk before you give it to the baby!

- Make sure the bottle you feed him is from the refrigerator and not one that has been lying around the house. The milk could have (ew! ick!) curdled.

- Cradle the baby in one arm and feed her the bottle. The best way to hold the baby is at a slight angle with her head elevated. You might want to put a pillow under the arm holding her.

- A baby will let you know if he isn't hungry. If he doesn't want the bottle, don't force it on him.

- If the baby starts to drink and then cries, check the nipple. It may be clogged.

- If you run out of milk or formula and the baby is crying for a bottle, you can fill it with water, or half apple juice and water (be sure and ask if it's all right to give the baby juice).

- Burp the baby after you feed her. Place a towel or cloth diaper over your shoulder, hold her upright against your shoulder, and firmly pat her back. Be patient. Sometimes it takes a little while for the burp to come up. (Give it about a minute.) Don't panic if she doesn't burp. Some don't need to.

SNACKS

You can never go wrong with peanut butter on a saltine or graham cracker. Carrot and celery sticks are crunchy and healthy. Apple and orange slices are also easy to handle and delicious. Top them off with a cup of milk or juice.

"What kind of snacks can I give a baby who only has a few teeth?"

Saltines
Graham crackers
Teething biscuits
Cheerios
Vanilla wafers

NOTE: Be careful with grapes, nuts, raisins, or hard candy. Really little kids can choke on them. Parents will usually advise you what they can or can't eat, but as a rule of thumb, if you're not sure the child is ready yet, don't give it to him!

KITCHEN SAFETY

- Turn handles of pans to face the wall or away from the edge of the stove when cooking. (Little ones can grab a handle and pull the pan off the stove.)

- If you are using the oven, be aware that the door and glass window in the door are HOT. Keep children away from the oven.

- Make sure the burners and stove are turned OFF when you are finished using them.

- Never set anything but a pot, pan, or kettle on a stove. Even if the burners are off.

- When using the microwave, do not put any metal bowls or objects in the oven.

- Always be careful when using knives around children, and be sure to store them out of their reach.

STACEY AND DAWN DO LUNCH

If you're up for making something a little more fun and different, here are some quick and easy recipes that are tasty and entertaining, courtesy of Dawn and Stacey.

ANTS ON A LOG

I know it sounds gross, but it's not. Kids love helping to make these, too. —Dawn

Ingredients: Celery
Cream cheese
Raisins

Directions: Wash the celery and cut it into bite-size pieces, about an inch long. Using a knife, fill the celery trough with cream cheese. Then you and the kids put the ants (raisins) on the log!

FRUIT AND CHEESE KABOBS

These are very healthy and fun to make. — Stacey

Suggested
Ingredients: Apple chunks
Grapes
Orange slices
Watermelon chunks
Cantaloupe slices
Cheese cubes
Toothpicks

Directions: Cut and peel whatever fruit you have on hand and put it into little bowls. Cut the cheese in small squares and put those in a bowl, too. Let the kids make their own kabobs by placing alternating colors and flavors onto their toothpicks.

(Since you are using toothpicks, be extra careful with tiny kids.)

SANDWICH ROLL-UPS

This is good for a snack or lunch. They're really colorful and delicious.
—Dawn

Ingredients: Rolling pin
Bread
Any filling:
    Cream cheese
    Tuna salad
    Egg salad
    Peanut butter and jelly

Directions: Cut off crusts and roll out the bread with the rolling pin until it's very flat. Cover the slice with whatever filling you choose, then roll it up like a rug.

SATURDAYS

A Saturday is the healthy equivalent of a sundae. Kids love to make them.
—Stacey

Ingredients: Pineapple rings
Banana
Yogurt or cottage cheese

Choice of toppings:
    raisins
    grated coconut
    granola
    chocolate chips or carob chips
    nuts

Directions: Place one or two pineapple rings in the bottom of a bowl. Cut the banana in half and place one half in each pineapple ring. Spoon cottage cheese or yogurt on top of the pineapple and banana and sprinkle with your favorite topping.

MONSTER TOAST

I know this is Dawn and Stacey's section and I'm usually a junk food fiend, but this is a really fun project to do with the kids. And it's pretty healthy.
                                              — Claudia

Ingredients: Whole wheat or white bread
                Milk
                Butter
                Food coloring
                Q-Tips

Directions: Toast bread and butter it. Mix a drop or two of food coloring in a couple of tablespoons of milk. Paint monster faces on to the bread with the Q-Tips.

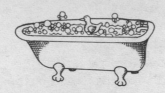

BATHTIME

"But I already took a bath last week..."

If you can get them from the living room to the bathroom, most kids enjoy bathtime. The problem is getting them into the bathtub.

I always make a game of it. First I announce that the S.S. Bath Tub will be leaving in fifteen minutes. That gives the kids time to get used to the idea. Then I make announcements at different intervals: "Ten minutes to bathtime." "Five minutes to bathtime." "I'm filling the bathtub." "The bubbles are here!"

— Kristy

I ask the kids to pick out some toys to take into the tub. I even stock my kid-kit with a few special squirter bath toys. That always does the trick!

— Claudia

BASIC TUB RULES

■ Gather your supplies ahead of time: towels, kid shampoo (one that doesn't sting their eyes), washcloth, and soap. That way you never have to leave the bathroom.

■ Run the water and test it. When you turn off the taps, turn off the cold water last in case the faucet drips.

■ NEVER LEAVE A CHILD ALONE IN THE BATHTUB. IF THE PHONE OR DOORBELL RINGS, DON'T ANSWER IT. A baby could slip under the water in a second's time. And an older child could stand up, slip, and hit his head.

WASHING HAIR

■ Wet hair with a washcloth. Squeeze a little bit of shampoo on your palm and then massage into scalp. Most kids (and adults) hate getting soap in their eyes. Be very careful not to let it drip down the child's face. Have a towel handy for him to press to his face in case it happens.

■ Rinsing is the difficult part. You can either run a wet washcloth from the forehead back to rinse (this takes several strokes and is good for little babies) or you can get it over with all at once. Ask him to tilt his head back and look at the ceiling. Then pour water over the hair. Again, have the towel handy to press to his face. If he hates getting his eyes wet (lots of kids do), ask him to hold a washcloth across his eyes before rinsing.

■ Be careful when kids get out of the tub. They generally have the urge to run around. Their feet are wet and they could easily slip on the tiles in the bathroom. Ask them to stand still on the rug until they are absolutely dried.

■ After the bath, be sure to let the water out of the tub and put the tub toys back where they came from. Hang up the towels and put the kids' clothes in the dirty clothes basket.

"How do I wash a baby?"

If the baby is really tiny, you should consider just giving him a sponge bath. Be sure to wash the baby's face, hands, and bottom with a washcloth. Put on a fresh diaper and put him into his PJs.

BEDTIME

"I don't wanna go and you can't make me!"

You've just shown that you're the most fun person on the planet. You've played great games, made delicious snacks, and bathtime was a blast. Now you want the kids to go to bed. Are they going to want to leave you to go to sleep? No way. UNLESS you make going to bed just as enjoyable an event as the rest of the evening.

■ Make a game of going to the kids' room.

I tell my charges to pretend we're bears lumbering off to our cave and then we crawl on all fours to the bedroom. I always make sure the kids know I'm going with them to their room. That I'm not just sending them off to bed.

—Kristy

- Kids can be pretty crafty when they start asking for that last drink of water or one more visit to the bathroom. Try to cover all those bases before you take them to their room.

IF YOU'VE WARNED THEM THAT BEDTIME IS APPROACHING, THEN YOU CAN SAY THINGS LIKE, "LAST CHANCE TO HAVE A GRAHAM CRACKER AND A GLASS OF MILK" OR "FINAL PIT STOP BEFORE BEDTIME."
— LOGAN

- Allow enough time for the children to relax into the rhythm of bedtime. Take them to their room. Dim the lights. Put on soothing music. You can sit with them in a rocking chair or sit next to their beds talking in a quiet voice. This bedtime ritual can easily take a half an hour to forty-five minutes.

I always read my charges a couple of good night stories. One of the best ones for little kids is _Goodnight Moon_ by Margaret Wise Brown. Then I warn them before I read the last book, "This is the last story, and when we're finished, I'm going to turn out the light."
— Mary Anne

- If the kids are really little, walk them around their room and let them say good night to their stuffed animals and the pictures on the walls before you put them in their beds.

35

my brother Squirt likes it when I sit for a while in the room with him after the lights are out. It's comforting for him to know that he's not being left by himself in the dark.

        — Jessi

BEDTIME FOR BABY

Usually babies get a little fussy around bedtime. That's how you know it's time to take them to their rooms. Most parents have a bedtime ritual (be sure and ask them what it is) but usually it involves:

- dimming the lights to just a night-light

- rocking the baby

- listening to soothing music

- feeding a bedtime bottle.

Some parents don't want their baby put to bed with a bottle, because dentists worry that it promotes tooth decay. If it's all right with the parents to do that, be sure you remove the bottle after the baby falls asleep. There's nothing worse than finding a curdled bottle of milk days later because it was hidden beneath the blankets.

Don't expect the baby to fall asleep right away. Allow some time (at least fifteen minutes to a half hour) for the bedtime ritual. Once the baby is asleep, spend a little more time in the room. Then tiptoe out, leaving the door ajar so you can hear if she wakes up. Some homes have baby monitors. Make sure the monitor and receiver are on and the monitor is placed where you can hear it.

"What if the baby cries?"

Sometimes babies cry a little and go back to sleep. Listen for a few minutes and if the crying continues:

■ Check to see if the baby is wet or tangled in her blankets.

Try patting the baby on the back and humming.

If a gentle back massage doesn't work, try picking her up and walking around the room with her, or rocking her.

If the crying persists, try the bottle again.

If crying is intense, check to see if a part of her clothing is bothering her. Take off her clothes and check for a sharp clothing tag, diaper pin, or string caught on her fingers or toes.

Sometimes they're just too hot. Removing a few layers of clothing often stops the crying.

Try changing location. Sometimes just walking into the bathroom and showing her her reflection in the mirror can stop a baby's tears.

Try putting the baby's hand under warm running water. Water is a great soother for everyone and may be enough to take her mind off crying.

If the crying *still* persists, the baby may be teething. The parents would probably warn you of this ahead of time, but they usually have a tube of Orajel or Num-Zit to numb the gums and take the pain away. You squeeze a little onto your finger and rub it gently on the baby's gums.

NOTE: If the crying is solid and goes on for an extremely long time (forty-five minutes to an hour) and no amount of comfort like rocking or a bottle will help, call the parents and ask for their advice.

NIGHTMARES

- Be sure a child who's had a nightmare is completely awake. That way the scary dream won't happen again. Talk in a reassuring voice as you explain to her that it was ONLY A DREAM.

- Turn on a dim light and show her that she's in her room with all of her favorite toys and she is safe and sound.

- As long as she's awake, it's a good idea to take her to the bathroom.

- When she's back in bed, try playing some soothing music or leaving on an extra light. Stay with her until she's gone back to sleep.

AFTER THE KIDS ARE ASLEEP

Okay, you've been a terrific baby-sitter. You've played with the children, fed and bathed them, and successfully put them to sleep. Now you're exhausted. Do you stretch out on the couch and watch TV? Not yet. There are a few things you need to do before you can take a break.

- Pick up the toys, put books back on the shelves, and generally straighten up any mess that the children left behind. (Even if they didn't do it while you were there, parents appreciate a tidy-looking place.) If the kids had dinner or a snack, make sure the dining table and counters are wiped clean and that the dishes are either washed or put in the dishwasher.

- Check on the children about every half hour.

- If you do make a phone call, try to limit the time (no longer than ten minutes). Remember, clients may be trying to call *you* to see how things are going, or to give you some last-minute instructions.

- Try to stay awake until midnight. If you are tired and feel like you must lie down, make sure you are within hearing range of the children.

"WHAT SHOULD I DO IF...?"

- **The phone rings.** Ask the parents how they would like the phone answered. "Hello, Henderson residence. I'm sorry, they're not here right now. May I take a message?"

- **The doorbell rings.** If the parents haven't told you they are expecting a visitor, then don't let anyone inside. Just say, "I'm sorry, Mrs. Henderson can't come to the door right now. Let me take your name and she can call you when she's available."

- **There's a delivery person at the door.** Ask them to leave the package outside the door (you can pick it up later).

- **There's a prowler outside.** If you hear sounds and are frightened, call a neighbor and ask them to check outside for you. If you can't reach a neighbor, call your local police, explain your situation, and ask for their advice.

WHEN THE PARENTS ARRIVE HOME

Parents love to hear about the cute things their children did or said. Be sure and tell them. It lets them know that you're paying attention and that you like their kids.

—Kristy

Be sure and let parents know if the children were acting sick or if they refused to eat their dinner.

—Shannon

"What if they're late—*hours* late?"

First, if it looks as if you're going to be late getting home, call your parents and explain the situation to them so they won't be worried. Sometimes clients just forget about the time. But if they're hours late, when they get home, tell them that you were worried. Ask them to call you the next time they are delayed. If you had told them that you couldn't stay out past midnight and they come home at one A.M., remind them that you needed to be home earlier.

"What if I don't think they should drive me home?"

If your clients seem to have had too much to drink and you don't feel good about their ability to drive you home, call your parents.

When they answer, say, "Mom, the Hendersons are home. You can come get me now."

"What if they don't have enough money to pay me?"

You may run into a situation where the clients are out of money or can't find their checkbook. If that's the case, then write up a quick bill stating the number of hours you worked, the date, and what they owe you. Be sure and write your name on the bill. If they forget to pay you within a week, make a phone call and give them a friendly reminder.

Sometimes clients don't have the correct change, so I always carry several one dollar bills and quarters with me just in case.
—Stacey

PART II
BABY-SITTING CLUBS

STARTING YOUR OWN
BABY-SITTERS CLUB

■

You and your friends really like to baby-sit and you really like each other. Now you want to form a club. Here's how:

1) **Choose officers.** A club means teamwork, and it helps if each person is assigned specific duties. Is one of you good at math? She'd make a great treasurer. Who is the most organized and has the best handwriting? You may want to elect that person secretary.

2) **Collect dues**, if necessary. Every business needs money to get started, though your Baby-sitters Club will be very inexpensive to launch. Dues cover the costs of transportation, photocopying fliers and business cards, and snacks at your regular meetings. Remember, once your club starts baby-sitting and earning money, you'll pay yourselves back in no time.

3) **Establish fees**. Decide on an hourly rate that everyone in the club will charge. You may want to ask for higher fees for more than one child, or have different rates for afternoons, evenings, and weekends.

4) **Keep records**. There are three separate records to keep. (See Part V in the back of this book.) You may want to make a different person responsible for each.

- **Maintain a client list.** Write down the client's name, address, phone number, the children's names and ages, and notes about their birthdays, pets, favorite foods, books, and games. Note special rules, bedtimes, allergies, and so on.
- **Keep an appointment book.** Record the name of the client, the time of the appointment, and the rate per hour. Note if the parents are picking you up or if you have to get there on your own.
- **Record your earnings.** It's fun to see the profits roll in!

5) **Advertise.** Print up fliers and have each club member distribute to her church or synagogue, doctor and dentist's office, supermarket, health club, laundromat, and children's stores.

BABY-SITTING CLUBS
AROUND THE COUNTRY

■

Did you know that there are over a thousand baby-sitting clubs in the United States? That includes Hawaii, Alaska, and Puerto Rico! Scholastic Inc. ran a survey and found that most of the club chapters have four to seven members who are between eleven and thirteen years old and have been baby-sitting for one to two years. We talked to the members of some of the clubs around the country to find out their secrets for success. Here's what they said:

IOWA CITY, IOWA

Noelle N. :	**President**
Laurie O.:	**Vice-President**
Liz C.:	**Secretary**
Michelle M.:	**Treasurer/Associate Member**

"We have nearly a hundred clients. We started advertising at our church and the word just spread!"

Best Advice: "Learn CPR. We have all taken a course and are certified."

Best On-the-Job Training: "We all baby-sat in our church's nursery and toddler room. We got lots of experience changing diapers and it really helped us learn how to handle babies."

Best Advertising Tip: "We hold coloring contests. A flier is attached to the drawing, so when the kids bring their picture home, the parents find out about our club."

Best Tip for the Kid-Kits: "We give out stickers if the kids are good and small prizes (not *too* little cause they could choke on them) if they're really good. Our prizes include bubbles and bubble wands, stamps and stationery items."

Best Group Activity: "We love to throw parties for our clients' kids. One of our themes was *The Little Mermaid*. But our favorite event was the Backyard Circus. We all dressed as clowns and played fun games like bowling and fishing."

Noelle

WARETOWN, NEW JERSEY

Erin V.:   President/Secretary

Carisa L.:   Vice-President/Treasurer

Robyn F.:   Junior Officer

"We are all CPR-certified and can handle children with special needs. We have three children with epilepsy, one who's autistic, two with diabetes, and a lot with asthma. We also know sign language."

Best Advice: "Take a Safe Sitter course. Emergencies do happen. I had to use the Heimlich maneuver on a child who was choking on an orange. I did the Heimlich and then the finger sweep to get it out of his throat. Boy, was I glad I knew what to do!"

To find out about a program in your area write:
SAFE SITTER • 1500 North Ritter Ave.• Indianapolis, IN 46219

Best Advertising Tip: "We passed out our cards at the doctor's office and one of the nurses hired us. After that people said, 'You baby-sit for a nurse? You must be good.' Now the doctors recommend us to all their patients, especially new parents."

Best Tip for New Clients: "Erin and I baby-sit for a new client together. That way we both get to know the children and parents at the same time."

Favorite Group Outing: "Erin and I volunteer at a nursing home and we love to take the kids there. We've made Valentine's cards and painted pumpkins and both the old folks and children really have a good time."

Carisa

49

☙THE BABY-SITTERS CLUB☙

ALEX. CITY, ALABAMA

Katie P.:	**President**
McKenzie T.:	**Vice-President**
Allison R.:	**Junior Officer**
Tracey B.:	**Alternate Officer**

"Our club gets together in the summers. That's when more people need sitters and when we have the most time."

Best Baby-sitting Tip: "Get a key from the parents! If you take the kids outside to play it's really easy to get locked out of the house. One little boy I sat for ran inside to use the bathroom and locked the front door. I was stuck outside with his brothers and sisters while he was inside. It was awful."

Favorite Activity: "We like to take our charges on field trips. One time we went to the Montgomery Zoo with a few of the parents. But our favorite thing to do is make up plays with the kids and then videotape them."

Best Group Event: "Our church holds a Parents' Night Out. All of the parents bring their kids to the church and a bunch of us watch them while the adults go and have a fun evening out."

Katie

BABIES + KIDS INC

SAN DIEGO, CALIFORNIA

Brenda S.:	**President**
Bethany O.:	**Vice-President**
Maldetta W.:	**Treasurer**
Jennifer R.:	**Secretary**
Recinah W.:	**Associate Member**
Ava T.:	**Honorary Member**
Yanina V.:	**Honorary Member**

"Our club started almost three years ago. We don't really hold separate BKI meetings because we see each other every week at Girl Scouts."

Best Tip: "Take a first-aid course. We did and earned a Girl Scout badge. Be sure and put on your fliers that you've had first aid."

Best Kid-Kit Ingredients: "Kids love read-along cassette tapes. Be sure and bring your tape recorder. We also stock stickers, notebook paper, safety scissors, and glue."

Favorite Baby-sitting Event: "Brownie Play Day. All of the troop mothers had a picnic lunch while we entertained the Brownies. We played musical chairs, sang songs, made yarn god's-eyes, and did face painting. It was a lot of fun and we earned a Girl Scout badge."

Bethany

PART III
DEAR ANN

LETTERS FROM MY READERS

■

Dear Reader,

Each year I receive about 14,000 letters from devoted readers of the Baby-sitters Club. A lot of them ask about the series and writing, but many of the letters contain very specific questions about baby-sitting. I thought you might like to know what problems other sitters face on the job and what kind of solutions are possible.

Good luck out there!
Ann

ALL MY CHILDREN

▼▼▼▼▼▼▼▼▼▼▼▼▼▼▼▼▼▼▼▼▼▼▼▼▼▼▼▼▼▼▼▼▼▼▼▼

Dear Ann,

Hi. I am twelve years old and I baby-sit four kids at once. A two-year-old, a four-year-old, a six-year-old, and an eight-year-old. When the eight-year-old wants to play house, the two-year-old wants to play dolls, and the four- and six-year-olds want to play army. How do I entertain them all at once?

Sincerely,
Jessi S.
Atlantic Highlands, NJ

▼▼▼▼▼▼▼▼▼▼▼▼▼▼▼▼▼▼▼▼▼▼▼▼▼▼▼▼▼▼▼▼▼▼▼▼

Dear Jessi,

Four children at once! You deserve a medal. One way to solve your problem is to plan activities that they all can do (at their own levels). If you bring coloring supplies in your Kid-Kit, the two-

55

year-old can color on blank paper, the four- and six-year-olds can fill coloring books, and the eight-year-old can design his own zoo or ocean. Just write the theme at the top of a piece of paper and he can fill in the animals. Try making hats out of newspapers. Color the hats and model them in front of the mirror (the two-year-old will probably like the mirror part best!). Use Play-Doh and cookie cutters. Tell everyone to make animal pretend food (make sure no one eats it. Ew ick!). Try time sharing. Make it fun. Set the kitchen timer for ten minutes—then spend time with each one doing the activity of his choice. Or let the children take turns choosing a game that everyone can play: Follow the Leader, Simon Says, or Karen Brewer's favorite, Let's All Come In. Speaking of Let's All Come in—guess what? My dad and his friends invented that game when they were little. They would play it and Dad always made his younger sister be the dog or take the parts no one else wanted, which she hated. Poor Aunt Adele never fails to remind Dad of this at family gatherings.

All the best,
Ann

BABY TALK

Dear Ann,

     I baby-sit a three-year-old who lives next door to me. Her mom is going to have another baby in less than a month. The girl I baby-sit hates the idea of her new baby (well, you know what I mean). She is usually a very active girl. Now when I baby-sit, all she wants me to do is read to her. What do I do?

Your #1 fan in NY, Kelli
Evans Mills, NY

Dear Kelli,

   Your three-year-old is going through a tough time. With all of the excitement about the new addition she probably feels she's being replaced. Her mom can't really hold her on her lap right now. Most likely her parents are focusing their energy on getting ready for the big event. It's very understandable that she wants you to sit by her and devote your full attention to her by reading. It's great that you can do that. Everything you can do now to let her know how special she is will help. Next time you visit, try bringing her a wrapped present in your Kid-Kit. It doesn't have to be a new toy, or anything big at all. The new baby is going to be receiving lots of presents and it's nice for her to get one, too. Do you have a doll in your Kid-Kit? Or does she have a baby doll? If her parents haven't already thought of it, you might want to suggest that they get her a baby that she can care for. They have inexpensive ones that come with bottles for pretend feeding. When the new baby arrives, and you are asked to baby-sit for both children, you two can take care of your babies together. Or ask her to be your helper—bring you diapers, help feed the baby, wind up the music box, find a toy for the baby to look at. There are also some very cute books that you could find in the library by Mercer Mayer dealing with the subject of getting a new baby sister. *Sesame Street* has some good books on this, too. Just ask your librarian.

All the best,
Ann

JUST SAY WHOA!

Hi!

    I have something that bothers me when I baby-sit for this one family. I baby-sit for two kids, well, actually I baby-sit for eight, but only get paid for baby-sitting two!! The father of the two kids I baby-sit knows they have all their friends over but still only pays for baby-sitting two. The parents of the other kids know when I baby-sit and it seems they only go over when I baby-sit. I don't want to go over to the kids' house and tell their parents to pay me for baby-sitting their kids, too! I just don't know what to do with all the kids. I'm only thirteen and I really can't handle that many kids all at once every day!!

T.C.
Lisle, IL

Dear T.C.,

    Eight kids is too much for anybody to handle. Even in professional day care centers, the maximum number of children the law allows one person to care for is six. You definitely need to speak to your client. Tell him that you take your job seriously and that eight children are too many for any one baby-sitter to care for properly. (Remember, the Pike family hires two sitters if they're leaving more than four of the kids at home.) It would probably be a good idea to tell the parents of the other children (in a note or on the phone) that you are the sole adult watching eight children each day. They may be surprised and dismayed. Kristy (Miss Great Ideas herself) would suggest that you offer your client a solution to this problem. Suggest that one or two of the other parents come *with* the kids when they visit. Also, it would be sharing the duties of host. For example: on Monday the six children (and a few of their parents) can come to your house. Tuesday, you take your charges to one of their homes. Wednesday, all of you visit a different host family.

It takes a little extra courage to speak up about these things but it's the good kind of courage, a forthrightness that you'll use the rest of your life. Remember, you're not complaining. You're just being a responsible baby-sitter and proving to your client that it was a great idea that he hired you to care for his kids. If you can't get up the nerve to talk to your client, ask one of your parents to do it. This is too big a problem to ignore.

All the best,
Ann

BARF-O-RAMA

Dear Ann M. Martin,

What do you do if you are baby-sitting an eight-month-old baby and a three-year-old and all of a sudden, the eight-month-old spits up. How do you keep the three-year-old entertained while you try to comfort the other kid? Please write! Thanks.

Sincerely,
Melisa
Fairfax Station, VA

Dear Melisa,

First of all, spitting up is normal for an eight-month-old, so don't panic. I know it's hard to stay calm when a baby is crying at the top of his lungs and a toddler is vying for your attention, but start by taking a deep breath and then speaking in a calm voice to the three-year-old. Explain the situation to him. You might want to ask him to help by bringing you a towel while you get a warm washcloth. That keeps him involved in the process. Tell the three-year-old that you need to sit quietly with the baby to calm her down. Offer the three-year-old a choice: Would he like to sit quietly with you in the bedroom, or would he rather watch a little TV or read a book while you go to the bedroom? If he feels like he's "in the loop" then I think you'll find him to be a good helper.

Sincerely,
Ann

NO GIRLS ALLOWED

Dear Ann,

I baby-sit for a little boy and he does not like it when I watch him take a bath. What should I do?

From,
Tiffany
Mechanicsburg, PA

Dear Tiffany,

Little children can get just as embarrassed as adults and should be given privacy if they ask for it. If he is old enough to be left in the bathtub by himself (ask his parents if they think he is) then I suggest you run his bath for him, provide him with a towel and washcloth, and then sit outside the door while he takes his bath. Tell him, "If you need me to wash your hair or help you get out, just let me know." I recommend keeping the door slightly ajar so you can hear if something goes wrong. Children appreciate it when adults knock before entering their bedroom or bathroom and ask permission to use a toy of theirs. If you treat them with courtesy, then (hopefully) they'll return the favor.

Sincerely,
Ann

AFTER HOURS

Dear Ann •••••••••••••••••••••••••••••••••••

    I have a seven-year-old girl who lives on my street. I have baby-sat for her and her three-year-old brother a couple of times. The problem is, she is always coming over to "play" with me. I have suggested more than once that she play with one of her friends her own age. She either says she likes me better or she invites her friends over, too. The mother sometimes sends the girl outside with her little brother and they end up coming to my house. When I walk the girl and her brother home because I am unable to watch them, the mother gets upset and wants to know what the kids did wrong, even though I've said they were fine, I just was too busy to watch them at that moment. Sometimes the parents walk the kids over and say, "Have a nice time, I'll be back soon." I'm not being paid to watch the girl or her brother even though I use up most of my Kid-Kit on them.

Help!
Erica 13
Mt. Laurel, NJ•••••••••••••••••••••••••••••••••••

Dear Erica,

It sounds as if you have done a lot of the right things. You've let the kids and parents know in a subtle and nice way that you're too old and too busy to play with them. Unfortunately, it sounds as though these people need something a little more direct. Try calling the parents and telling them how much you enjoy baby-sitting for their kids but that you have a problem— you're too old to be their playmate and you're not sure how to let the kids know this without hurting their feelings. Ask for the parents' advice on what to do. Hopefully the parents will get the point and talk to the kids themselves. If this doesn't work, then it's time for the sledgehammer approach. Tell the parents that you need to be paid for baby-sitting and that it would be helpful if they made arrangements with you before they sent their kids over to your house. I know this is hard to say to an adult. But most people appreciate an honest, straightforward person. They may not even be aware that they are taking advantage of you. Have you told your parents? If you find it too difficult to tell the kids' parents yourself, see if you can have your mom or dad talk to them for you. One thing for sure, don't let it ride. Speak up. It's the only way to solve the problem.

All the best,
Ann

LOVE AT FIRST BITE

✏️ Dear Ann,
I baby-sit for a nine-month-old baby that is teething and it cries all the time. I gave it a teething ring but the baby won't be quiet. What should I do?

Your number 1 fan, Erin
Del City, OK

Dear Erin,

Teething is a miserable experience for everyone—the baby and the sitter. There are some products that automatically make the baby feel better. Talk to your client and see if she uses Num-Zit or Orajel and if it's all right for you to rub some on the baby's gums. It numbs their gums and relieves the soreness instantly. The proper dosage of baby Tylenol will also help with the pain. Again, ask the parent if and when it's all right to administer it (remember: never give any medicine, prescription or not, without getting explicit instructions from the parents first). Some babies don't really like teething rings but they do like chewing on something. A saltine cracker or teething biscuit is good for them to gnaw on. Some babies like to chew on a cool, wet washcloth or a dill pickle (make sure it's a whole one, so they can't pull off chunks and choke on it). When they're teething, the pressure can be really great on their gums and sitting up or lying on their stomach may not feel good. Babies sometimes like to lie on their backs, arching their heads back over your arm. Try rocking them to sleep that way.

Good luck,
Ann

FRIGHT NIGHT

Dear Ann,

I baby-sit for my cousin. She's really a great kid but she's terrified of two things. Thunder and lightning. Every time she hears thunder or sees lightning, she screams. She's afraid the lights are going to go out. And she is scared of the dark. What do I do?

Fondly, Mari C-R
Los Angeles, CA

Dear Mari,

One way to help your cousin is to make a game of being in a thunderstorm. Start by building a fort out of blankets and a table and chairs. Crawl into the dark space with flashlights and pretend that a storm is taking place. You can make up funny stories about what could happen when it's raining out. Talk to your local librarian about some easy-to-read books that explain what thunder and lightning are. Once your cousin knows more about it, maybe she won't be so scared. There's also a lovely book by Robert McCloskey called *Time of Wonder* that you might like to read to her. One passage describes a really neat summertime storm. It might be fun to make a "Thunderstorm Kit." Get a box and fill it with a flashlight, some snacks to eat, maybe an old watch with a second hand for timing the seconds between the flash of light and the sound of thunder (that gives you a rough idea of how many miles away the storm is). To work on her fear of the dark, try getting her used to being in dark places. Hide in the closet together or play in a darkened room (but always keep a flashlight close by!).

Good luck,
Ann

CAUGHT IN THE MIDDLE

Dear Ann,

What do you do when one kid (age three) wants to go outside and the other (age five) wants to stay and play inside?

Your biggest fan,
Elizabeth T.
Bigfork, MT

Dear Elizabeth,

This is a difficult question because neither of these children should be left on her own. I think the best way to handle this situation is to take turns. Spend a half hour outside and a half hour inside. Let each one be in charge of the activities for her half hour. If you take the kids outside in cold weather make sure they are dressed properly. Their heads and ears should be covered and they should probably be wearing gloves. (It's not a bad idea for you to tuck a handful of Kleenex in your pocket to take care of the runny noses that invariably appear in cold weather.) If it's a very warm, sunny day, you may want to consider applying sunscreen. Always ask the parents before they leave if it's all right to take the children outside.

Sincerely,
Ann

KEEP IT CLEAN

Hi, Ann,

What do you do if the client you're baby-sitting for asks you to clean the whole house and doesn't pay for doing it?

Your #1 Fan,
Chrissy
North Bergen, NJ

Dear Chrissy,

Picking up toys, straightening the kids' rooms and living room, and washing dishes that were used that evening is generally part of a baby-sitter's job. Parents really appreciate returning to a tidy house. However, general cleaning is an added duty and should be rewarded. One summer I baby-sat for a family and also did light housekeeping, but I was paid extra for the housekeeping. We agreed on that from the very beginning. Dawn had a problem like yours in the book, *Dawn and the Impossible Three*. The Barrett house was a mess and so one day, Dawn and the kids cleaned it up. Then Mrs. Barrett started assuming that Dawn would clean the house every time she baby-sat. Mrs. Barrett deliberately left stacks of dirty dishes and heaps of laundry for Dawn to clean. Finally Dawn had to talk to Mrs. Barrett about it. She told her that she enjoyed sitting for Marnie, Buddy, and Suzi but she couldn't do all of her housework without being compensated. They finally came to the agreement that Mrs. Barrett would make a list of the chores she wanted done and would pay Dawn extra for doing them. I know it's difficult to be straightforward with an adult but maybe if you wrote down what you considered to be normal duties that go along with baby-sitting, and chores that you consider extra—it would be easier to discuss. Your client may not realize that she is taking advantage of you.

Good luck,
Ann

PARTY ON!

Dear Ann,

I want to have a baby-sitting party with my friends and some of the kids I sit for. Do you have any ideas on what we should do?

Jacqui
Lynn, MA

Dear Jacqui,

I've always found that outdoor activities are best for kids. If you're planning your party for winter, think about building snowmen and have a box of old clothes to dress the kids' creations. A sledding party is always fun. You don't have to use real sleds—they can be trays or Hefty bags or cardboard boxes. I like to make snow angels. A Swedish snowball tree is beautiful and can be made by creating a circle of snowballs, then stacking them up in smaller and smaller circles to create a tree. If you are planning a summer get-together, think about relay races, and silly games like Pass the Orange (you play this by holding an orange under your chin and passing it to your neighbor without using your hands). Scavenger hunts and treasure hunts can fill up the entire party. A piñata, filled with goodies, is fun. Pizza is easy and can feed lots of people. As you plan your party try to keep your kid/adult ratio to no more than three to one. Also, remember that children have short attention spans and an hour and a half is a perfect length for a party.

Have fun!
Ann

MAKING CHOICES

Dear Ann,

For the past year and a half, I have had a steady baby-sitting job on Saturday nights. However, lately I find that being tied up every Saturday night conflicts with plans my friends and I make. I don't want to lose this job but I want to be with my friends, too. What should I do?

Becky
Sudbury, MA ••••••••••••••••••••••••••••

Dear Becky,

Finding a sitter for Friday and Saturday nights is one of the toughest problems a parent faces. They know that teens need a social life and would fully understand if you told them about your problem. One solution might be for you to share the job with another sitter by alternating Saturday nights. That would allow you two nights a month with your friends and two nights with your clients' children. It sounds as though you've established a good relationship with your clients and I'm sure they'd be very happy if they knew you would still sit for them during the week and some Saturday nights.

Sincerely,
Ann

HERE A KID, THERE A KID, EVERYWHERE A KID KID

Dear Ann,

I signed up to help at my church's Sunday school. I was assigned to a class of about 20 five-year-olds. I'm supposed to bring in quiet games, toys, or books that they can play with. I was also wondering how to give your attention to the whole class. Five-year-olds love attention, and they're really possessive. (All the ones I've dealt with are!)

Thanks,
Jen
Simi Valley, CA

Dear Jen,

Taking care of 20 five-year-olds is as big a job as a teacher managing an entire kindergarten class. In order to do that, he or she usually has to do some preparation. You might want to arrive early and set up six or seven "play stations" with an activity already laid out, such as blocks enough for three, crayons and pictures to color, three puzzles, Play-Doh and cookie cutters, or Legos. Then assign different teams of three to each table and set a timer. Every ten or fifteen minutes, when the timer goes off, the team moves to a new station. There are also group games that can be played relatively quietly. Statues and Telephone are good ones. Sitting in a circle and singing songs like "This Old Man," "The Wheels on the Bus," or "The Hokey Pokey" get everyone involved without being too noisy. Find fun books that you can read aloud to everyone, and have the kids take turns holding up the pictures.

All the best,
Ann

SICK LEAVE

Dear Ann,

Hi! I'm twelve years old and I've been baby-sitting since I was almost eleven. One time when I was baby-sitting, I got sick and had to leave the kids with my mom, and ever since then I've been embarrassed to talk to my client. What's wrong with me?

Bonnie
Williamsburg, VA

Dear Bonnie,

Nothing's wrong with you. Baby-sitting is a big responsibility and it sounds as though you had quite a scare. But you rose to the occasion. You were sick and couldn't care for the children—

and you solved the problem: You called your mother and she took care of them. You didn't let your client down. You handled the situation like a responsible adult. It's all right to ask for help. Problems usually arise when people DON'T ask for help.

Sincerely,
Ann

NOTE: For future reference, if you've accepted a job but are starting to feel sick, call your clients and tell them *before* you show up to work. Most likely your clients would rather schedule someone else than risk exposing their children to an illness.

TOO CLOSE FOR COMFORT

Dear Ann,

I would like to know what to do if you're baby-sitting a kid one year younger than you! I got a new client (thanks to my mom) and she wants me to watch her ten-year-old son! (I'm eleven.) What should I do? Thanks!

Your #1 fan,
Cynthia G.
Philadelphia, PA

Dear Cynthia,

This is a situation that will take some delicate handling. I'd start by suggesting that your client refer to you as a friend who's coming to stay with her son, rather than as a "baby-sitter." That will save him the embarrassment of feeling like a baby. Because you are so close in age, he would probably really appreciate it if you act like a guest in his house. Ask him if it would be all right if you had a soda to drink and offer to pour him a glass, etc.

If his mother has given strict instructions that he disregards, explain that his mother has asked you to abide by her rules and in order to do that, you're going to need his help. If you two go to the same school, try not to mention that you're his baby-sitter. This could be the beginning of a nice friendship.

All the best,
Ann

CALL WAITING

Dear Ann,

The lady I usually baby-sit for has suddenly stopped calling me. Also, I found out that she had asked someone else to baby-sit for her the other day. As far as I know I have never done anything wrong to her. Should I call her and confront her about it? I'm really upset.

Sincerely,
Kara
Richmond, TX

Dear Kara,

Confront is an awfully harsh word. It implies that you're going to have an argument. I think talking to your client is an excellent idea, but you don't want to go into the discussion with a bad attitude. You might want to call and ask her if there is a time that you could come by and chat with her. Face-to-face is always best. When you get to her house, tell her that you've enjoyed baby-sitting for her and hope to continue. Rather than asking why she hasn't called, tell her that you'd like to know what you can do to improve your skills, because you'd like to be the best sitter possible. That is the point where she can bring up anything that has been bothering her. If she says you are just fine, then you can tell her you've noticed she hasn't called lately and you just want to make sure you haven't made any mistakes you didn't know about. Be sure and let her know you're still eager and ready to work for her. Remember, you need to approach this conversation maturely and positively. You may discover that she called that other baby-sitter because she wanted to branch out a little. From a client's perspective, it's a little scary to depend on just one sitter for everything.

Good luck,
Ann

NEW SITTER ON THE BLOCK

Dear Ann,

I haven't started baby-sitting yet only because my mom wants me to take a class first. I am taking one in October but my sister is older and she has been baby-sitting for a long time and I just know she will get all of the jobs and I won't. I don't think it is really fair but she is more experienced. What should I do so I can get a baby-sitting job?

Alison
San Marcos, CA

Dear Alison,

If your sister already has her own clients, don't try to compete with her. Find your own. Talk to your teachers or put up a notice at your church or temple. It would also be a good idea to give your sister's clients a call to tell them that if your sister is unable to sit for them, you are now trained and eager to start baby-sitting. There will probably come a time when your sister will choose to go to a movie with friends or a dance, rather than baby-sit. So being younger can be an advantage. I know from all of my friends who have children that there are never enough baby-sitters. It's just a matter of getting the word out.

Sincerely,
Ann

PART IV

HOUSEHOLD AND MEDICAL EMERGENCIES AND FIRST AID

HOUSEHOLD EMERGENCIES

■

Remember, "BE PREPARED!" is an important motto for baby-sitters to follow. And there's nothing more important than being prepared for a medical or household emergency. Familiarize yourself with the information in this section so you'll be ready before a crisis happens.

NOTE: Be sure and ask the parents to show you the location and contents of their first aid kit before they leave.

The important thing in all emergencies is to remain calm. Your number-one concern is the safety of you and the children. So if an emergency arises, take a deep breath, make sure all of you are out of harm's way, and then call for help.

FIRE

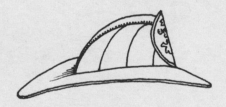

1) Do NOT try to put out the fire.

2) Get the children out of the house.

3) Go to the neighbors and call 911 or the fire department.

POWER OUTAGE

1) If the power is out in only part of the house, it's probably a fuse or a breaker. That is not dangerous. Let the parents deal with it when they get home.

2) If the power is out all over, find a flashlight or candles and matches. If you light a candle, be very careful of small children. Remember to keep the matches in your pocket and never leave a child alone with a lighted candle.

3) Be sure and turn off any appliances.

4) Call the electric company and let them know that your power is out.

5) The dark can be scary for kids so reassure them that the darkness is only temporary. You might want to make an adventure of it. Pretend you are sitting around a campfire in the middle of a beautiful forest.

STORMS

1) Be sure and stay inside with the children.

2) If the wind is particularly strong, keep the children away from the windows.

MEDICAL EMERGENCIES
■

DOS AND DON'TS OF MEDICAL EMERGENCIES

■ **DO** remain calm. It's the best thing you can do to help a hurt child. She'll see that you are relaxed and won't be quite so scared.

■ **DO** no harm. If something has gone wrong and you are not sure what to do, call for help rather than doing something that may be more harmful to the child.

■ **DON'T** move a child who has fallen and may be seriously hurt.

■ **DON'T** give any medication, even Tylenol, unless you have been given permission by the parents. (Aspirin should never be given to children because of its association with Reye's syndrome.)

■ **DO** call 911 (or an ambulance) *immediately* if:

   1. A child is unconscious.
   2. A child has trouble breathing or has stopped breathing.
   3. A child has been severely burned.
   4. A child has lost a lot of blood.

HOW TO CALL FOR HELP

If an emergency arises you'll need to be ready to call one of these numbers:

1) 911 (This emergency service is a hotline for the hospital, police, and fire department.) If 911 is not available in your community, you'll have to call an ambulance, the police, or the fire department directly. Make sure those numbers are in your book.

2) Poison Control Center

3) The parents

4) The family's doctor

"What do I say?"

1) Take a deep breath and speak slowly when an operator answers.

2) Explain your emergency: "Hello, I'm baby-sitting a child who has fallen down the stairs and is unconscious."

3) The operator will ask you where you are located. Give him your name and the address, phone number, and last name of the client in a slow, clear voice.

4) If he doesn't tell you what to do, ask what you should do until help arrives. Listen carefully.

5) Often an operator will ask you to remain on the line while he transfers you to a doctor who can give you more specific instructions. Don't hang up until you are told to do so.

"What do I do with the other kids when I'm handling an emergency?"

1) If the situation is very serious and requires you to call an ambulance, briefly let the kids know that their sister is sick, but you are calling for help and she'll soon feel a whole lot better.

2) If the other kids are capable of helping, give them a task to calm them down. Ask them to bring you the Band-Aids, a clean towel, or ice from the fridge.

3) Don't hold a crying baby when you call a doctor for advice. It will be difficult for the doctor to hear you and for you to hear her. Take a moment to strap her into the high chair or a walker or put her in the crib. It's okay to let her cry as long as she's safely out of harm's way.

"What do I say to the hurt child?"

A hurt child is frightened. He doesn't know what's happened to him or why he is hurting.

1) The best thing you can do is explain to him very simply what's happened. Let him know that his mom and dad are on their way and soon he'll feel all better.

2) Be sure to compliment him on his bravery. Tell him how proud you are that he fell down and only cried a little bit.

3) Blood is a scary thing for a child. If you are grabbing a washcloth, reach for a dark one so the blood won't show up so much.

4) If the situation isn't *too* serious, try making light of things. Joke about what a great story Jason's going to be able to tell at school the next day.

5) If the child's crying, ask him to whistle. You can't cry and whistle at the same time. Laugh with him as he tries to do it.

EMERGENCY FIRST AID

■

You can feel confident that ninety-nine times out of a hundred, nothing resembling a crisis will happen while you are baby-sitting. But if an emergency does arise, you should be prepared to deal with it.

This section provides quick, basic information on dealing with a variety of emergency situations. This is not a complete guide to first aid. It does not cover techniques for artificial respiration. That is a skill which should be learned in a First Aid or CPR class. For a more complete guide to first aid, take a look at books published by authoritative organizations such as the American Medical Association or the American Red Cross.

BREATHING DIFFICULTY

■ If a baby or child has stopped breathing, chances are likely that something is blocking the air passage. Check her throat and then CALL 911 (OR AN AMBULANCE) IMMEDIATELY.

Here's how to check for a blocked air passage:

Lay the baby or child on a flat, firm surface and tilt her head up in the sniffing position (where the jaw is a little bit forward). Check her mouth to see if anything is in her throat. If something is, do a sideways sweep with your finger to remove the object.

CHOKING

Choking can be very scary. The important thing is to try to remain calm and get out whatever is blocking the airway. It's usually a bite of food, a bottle cap, or a small toy. It can even be a piece of paper. If a child can cough, it generally means he's able to get the object out. But if the coughing is feeble, or he is gasping for breath or turning blue around the lips, he's definitely choking and you need to act fast.

■ Stop the choking BEFORE you call the doctor.

■ If the foreign object is in the throat and you can see it, try to hook it out with a finger. SWEEP SIDEWAYS so that you don't push the object back down the throat.

Baby or Small Child

1) Put a baby or small child facedown across your lap. His head should be lower than the rest of his body. Give him four quick slaps between the shoulder blades with the heel of your hand.

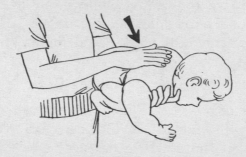

2) If this is not working, turn the child faceup across your lap, still keeping the head lower than the rest of the body. Give four quick chest thrusts on the sternum between the nipples with two or three fingers. Your fingers should run up and down the sternum rather than across it.

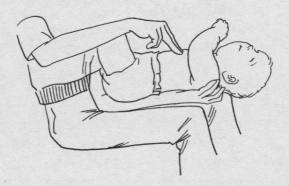

3) Continue alternating back slaps and chest thrusts until the object is dislodged, or help arrives.

For an Older Child, Use the Heimlich Hug

1) Stand behind him and wrap your arms around his waist.

2) Make a fist with one hand and clasp it with the other.

3) Place the fist against the child's stomach, slightly above the navel, below the midpoint of the rib cage.

4) PRESS into the stomach with a quick upward thrust.

5) Repeat at short intervals, if necessary, until the object pops out of the mouth.

6) If you've tried the Heimlich over and over and slapped him on the back, and nothing works, CALL 911 (OR AN AMBU-LANCE). Then continue trying to dislodge the object until help arrives.

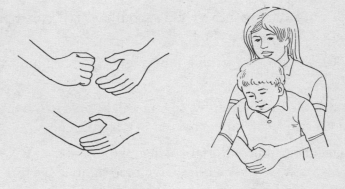

THE IMPORTANCE OF TAKING A CPR COURSE CAN-NOT BE STRESSED ENOUGH. IN AN EMERGENCY SUCH AS CHOKING, YOU DO NOT WANT TO HAVE TO THINK, YOU NEED TO KNOW. AND THAT COMES WITH TRAINING.

CONVULSIONS

If a child's body stiffens and she shakes uncontrollably, she may be having a convulsion. Sometimes her eyes can roll back into her head during the seizure. Convulsions in small children are usually caused by a rapid rise in temperature due to a bad infection, or they can be due to a specific medical condition such as epilepsy. They may also be a symptom of poisoning. They're very scary to watch, but the important thing is not to panic. A convulsion is generally not life-threatening and usually over very quickly.

DOS AND DON'TS FOR CONVULSIONS

■ **DO** clear the area of any objects that might hurt the child.

■ **DON'T** put anything into a child's mouth or try to pry open the teeth if they are clenched.

■ **DON'T** try to stop the jerking movements. You could hurt the child.

■ **DO** watch the child carefully, so you will be able to tell the doctor exactly what happened and in what order.

■ **DO** make the child comfortable when the convulsion has stopped. Make sure her clothes aren't too tight. If she feels extremely warm, undress her to her underwear. Then wet a washcloth and gently rub it across her forehead.

CALL THE DOCTOR. THEN CALL THE PARENTS.

ELECTRICAL SHOCK

Kids are often attracted to electrical outlets (especially ones without the protective caps). Unfortunately, contact with household electricity can cause burns. And the shock from the electricity may even cause unconsciousness or stop a child's breathing. If a child has stuck something in an electrical outlet or a baby has bitten through an electric cord and the child is still in contact with the electricity, the important thing is not to touch him directly. First:

1) Shut off the power.

2) If that's not possible, break the contact between the child and the electrical source, but not with your bare hands. If you touch either one directly, you could receive a shock. Use a wooden broom handle or plastic baseball bat, or wrap your arm in a coat and bat the cord away. Don't use anything that's wet or made out of metal. You could even grab a stiff pillow to shove the child away from the current.

3) After you have moved him away from the current, CALL 911 (OR AN AMBULANCE) AND THE PARENTS.

POISONING

If a child has eaten or drunk something poisonous or something you THINK might be poisonous, call a doctor immediately. Even if you've only found an empty container of pills lying near the child and you suspect he might have taken them, CALL A DOCTOR.

1) Ask the child to show you what he ate or drank.

2) Find the container.

3) Hold the container in your hand while you call the doctor or Poison Control Center.

4) Tell them what you think the child has swallowed. Describe the child's behavior and anything that seems unusual to you (such as a strange smell or stain on the child's clothing).

5) Follow instructions *exactly*. The person who answers your call may tell you to give the child water or milk to dilute the poison.

Or he may ask you to try to make the child vomit. Usually that's done with syrup of Ipecac, which would be kept in the medicine cabinet.

6) After you've done everything the Poison Control Center or the doctor tells you to do, CALL THE PARENTS.

Poison in the Eyes

If a poisonous substance has gotten into the child's eyes, hold his head over the sink, being careful to cover his nose and mouth, and flush his eyes continuously with lukewarm water.

POSSIBLE INDICATIONS OF POISONING

1) Vomiting and diarrhea

2) Burns around mouth (from drinking a corrosive poison)

3) Convulsions

4) An empty or open container known to hold poison or medicine lying near your child. Take this as a serious problem. Even if the child isn't acting sick, he could get sick.

5) Poisonous plant or berries in his hand or near him if he's unconscious

NOTE: The most common causes of poisoning are medicines, plants, personal care products (such as makeup and fingernail polish remover), and household cleaners.

UNCONSCIOUS CHILD

If a child is unconscious, CALL 911 (OR AN AMBULANCE) IMMEDIATELY. A head injury, electric shock, choking, convulsions, or ingestion of medicine or poison can all result in unconsciousness. There are also varying stages of unconsciousness. Sometimes a child can stagger around as if he is drunk, or he may act very confused and have blurred vision and then lapse into unconsciousness. Be sure to note his behavior and report it to the doctor.

1) First try to rouse him by pinching an earlobe or, in the case of a baby, tap him on the bottom of his feet.

2) Ask the child a question and give him time to respond.

3) If he doesn't respond, tilt his head back and check to see if he is breathing. Place your ear near his mouth. Listen for his breath and watch the chest to see if it rises and falls. If he isn't breathing, check to see if anything is blocking the air passage. If something is, use the Heimlich or methods described for choking to clear his throat.

4) If the child has fallen and is unconscious, DON'T MOVE HIM. You could do irreparable damage by moving his head or body. CALL 911 (OR AN AMBULANCE) and then cover him with a blanket and make sure he doesn't choke on any vomit or saliva.

BASIC FIRST AID
■

BEE STING

A sting from a wasp or a bee can really hurt, but you can stop the pain. Have your child sit in a chair and take deep breaths to remain calm.

1) If the stinger is still in the wound, remove it as quickly as possible by scraping it with a fingernail, or something clean—a knife, nail file, or even the edge of a driver's license or credit card. The important thing is not to pinch the stinger because it has a little sack that squirts more venom into the wound if it's squeezed.

2) Try to reduce the pain and swelling with a washcloth filled with ice, or even a can of cold soda pop pressed directly against the sting.

3) Here are two household products that will help get rid of the pain:

    a) Accent meat tenderizer—mix up a small paste with water and dab it on the sting. This will draw out the poison and lessen the pain.

    b) Baking soda and water—use about a teaspoonful of baking soda and a drop or two of water—just enough to make a thick paste that sticks to the skin.

IT'S AN EMERGENCY IF: The area swells quickly, with large, red, raised welts, the child's eyes become puffy, and he has diffi culty breathing. These signs would indicate an allergic reaction. CALL 911 (OR AN AMBULANCE) IMMEDIATELY.

BROKEN BONES AND FALLS

Kids are going to fall down. It's just part of growing up. But occasionally they sprain a wrist or ankle and sometimes they break a bone. Sometimes it's obvious that a bone has been broken and sometimes it's not so easy to tell. When in doubt it's best to treat the injury as if there's been a break.

1) Keep the child still and warm and don't move her unless it's absolutely necessary.

2) If the child is in a great deal of pain and you suspect a break, CALL THE PARENTS.

3) If a bone is sticking out of the skin, CALL 911 (OR AN AMBULANCE).

4) While you wait for help to arrive, you can apply a towel with ice in it or a bag of frozen vegetables from the freezer to cut down on the pain and stop some of the swelling.

BUMPS AND BRUISES

At some point during your baby-sitting career a kid will probably run into the edge of the counter, fall against the coffee table, or bonk her head on the floor or another kid. It just goes with the territory. These hurts are easy to take care of and mostly require a lot of sympathy. For minor bumps and bruises:

1) Apply something cold from the refrigerator to the bump. If you don't have ice to put in a washcloth, a bag of frozen vegetables or can of frozen juice will do. You can even use a can of soda pop from the fridge.

2) If the items from the freezer are too cold to hold against the injury, wrap them in a washcloth or dishtowel.

Split Lip

This is probably the most common injury you'll find in kids who are still a little unsteady on their feet.

1) Pat the lip with a cold washcloth and allow him to hold the washcloth to his mouth. You might want to put an ice cube in the washcloth and hold it there with a rubber band.

2) If you can find a Popsicle in the freezer, this is a yummy way to stop the pain and forget about the hurt lip.

3) CALL THE PARENTS if the split is bigger than a small cut or extends past the lip outline. It may need a stitch.

BURNS

Most burns that kids get are from touching hot electrical appliances like the stove or the dryer or an iron. They usually end up to be minor or moderate burns and can be dealt with by you, the baby-sitter. It's only in the case of a major burn, a chemical or an electric burn, that you need to call for help. Here's how to recognize the three types of burns:

MINOR (First Degree) : The affected area is red, like a bad sunburn.

MODERATE (Second Degree): Any burn that blisters.

MAJOR (Third Degree): Several layers of skin have been burned and it possibly covers a large area, which may appear very white. Usually the child has no severe pain because the nerves and vessels have been damaged.

What to do for a Minor Burn

1) Hold the burned area under cold running water for ten to fifteen minutes or until the pain goes away.

2) If the child won't hold the burned area under water, give him a glass or bowl of cold water (not ice water) that he can soak his hand in.

3) Raise the affected area so blood flow to the area is slowed down, which will make it less painful. For example, if a child has burned his wrist, raise his arm.

4) Call the parents.

5) Call the doctor if the area is covered in blisters or if the burned area is larger than the child's hand.

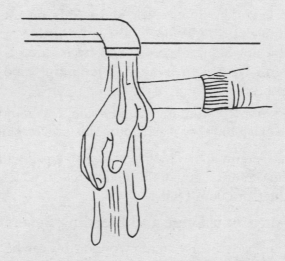

What to do for a Major Burn

If a large area of the body is burned, CALL 911 (OR AN AMBULANCE) immediately.

DOS AND DON'TS FOR BURNS

- **DON'T** apply anything to the burn, especially not butter.

- **DON'T** break a blister.

- **DON'T** remove clothes if they're stuck to the skin.

- **DO** flush with lots of water if it is a chemical burn and immediately remove any clothing that the chemicals are touching.

- **DO** call 911 (or an ambulance) if the burn is chemical or electrical, or if it covers a large area.

CUTS AND SCRAPES

Kids spend half their lives with Band-Aids on their knees or elbows, but seeing the blood is always a little scary. You can help them by not being alarmed and by making a big deal of how much fun wearing a Band-Aid is going to be. For minor cuts and scrapes:

1) Clean the wound by running it under cool water and patting it dry with a clean towel or washcloth. This prevents infection.

2) Put a Band-Aid on it, or a moist clean gauze pad with adhesive tape. If you can't find any of these, use a clean white sock, handkerchief, or white T-shirt.

If the Cut is Large and Bleeding Severely:

1) Press a clean pad directly on the wound (this can be a towel, or even a disposable diaper—it's clean and absorbent). Apply pressure for two to five minutes. If you can't find any cloth or a diaper, use your hand. This will slow the bleeding.

2) If blood soaks through the cloth, don't lift the dressing up—it

will start the bleeding all over again. Instead, apply another cloth over the old cloth and maintain the pressure.

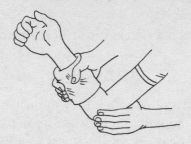

3) CALL 911 (OR AN AMBULANCE).

4) Keep the hurt area raised to slow down the bleeding and maintain pressure on the wound.

DO NOT APPLY A TOURNIQUET.
They are an extreme measure and dangerous!!!!!

DOG BITE

A bite from Rover (or even sister Sally) can be pretty painful. The important thing is to clean the wound and try to make the hurt go away. If a strange dog bit your charge, get a description of the dog, call a neighbor, and ask him to look for it. This is so the authorities can check to see if the dog has rabies. Meanwhile, here's what you do for a dog or human bite:

1) Thoroughly wash the wound with soap and water to remove any dirt or saliva.

2) Apply antiseptic cream.

3) Put a Band-Aid or sterile gauze pad over the bite.

4) To stop the pain, apply ice (over the bandage) and elevate the arm or leg.

5) Call the parents. If it's a severe bite, call the doctor.

EARACHE

Kids get lots of ear infections when they are little. You can usually tell when a baby has an earache because he is fussy and possibly pulling or rubbing his ear. Everyone knows an earache is painful. So if your charge is complaining of an earache or you think the baby might have one:

1) Call the parents and ask what to do. (They may recommend giving infant Tylenol.)

2) Try to stop the hurt. Fill a hot water bottle with hot water and wrap it in a towel. Tell the child to lie with his head on the towel. That will make the ear feel a little better.

3) If lying down makes the ear hurt more, make up a bed in a comfortable chair so he can sit upright.

4) Try asking the child to drink water or juice. Swallowing helps the clogged tubes in the ear open up. And clear tubes mean less pain.

DO NOT PUT ANYTHING IN THE EAR,
NOT EVEN A COTTON SWAB.

FEVER

A body temperature of 98.6°F to 100°F is generally normal for children. Anything over 100°F is considered a fever. Besides feeling very warm to the touch, a child with a fever may be glassy-eyed, have a flushed face, and breathe shallowly. A fever can be a sign that she is getting a cold or the flu or has an ear infection. If you suspect a fever:

1) Call the parents.

2) Try to reduce the temperature by taking off any clothes that may be making her hot. Once she's in her underwear, put her to bed and cover her with a light sheet.

3) If the temperature is between 102°F and 104°F , you might try giving a sponge bath on her arms and legs with lukewarm water until the parents get home.

4) Encourage the child to drink lots of water or juice.

HOW TO USE THE TEMPERATURE STRIP

■ A glass thermometer can be tricky with little kids. If the parents ask you to take the child's temperature, the easiest method to use on small children and babies is the temperature strip.

■ Hold it firmly across his forehead for fifteen seconds.

■ The color will move from block to block. The one that is brightest green is the child's temperature.

NOSEBLEED

A nosebleed can be caused by a bump on the nose, by a child picking his nose, or by some foreign object in the nose. It may bleed a lot and look terrible but assure the child that noses just do that. A nosebleed is rarely a serious problem. Here's what you do:

1) Sit the child down with his head over a sink or a bowl held in his lap. (Don't put the head back because this will cause the blood to run down his throat.)

2) Then pinch the tip of the nose with your finger and thumb firmly (but not too hard) for five minutes. (Be sure and look at the clock and stick to the five minutes.)

NOTE: If bleeding continues for more than thirty minutes and the child is getting dizzy, then you need to CALL A DOCTOR.

Object in Nose or Ear

Little kids have been known to shove popcorn kernels, beads, beans, Legos, or anything small enough to fit into their ears and noses. If this happens and the object seems too difficult to remove, CALL THE PARENTS, then CALL A DOCTOR.

1) If the object is in the nose and the child is old enough to understand, ask him to hold the open nostril closed and blow through the clogged one. (If she is very young, don't ask her to blow because she may sniff in first and the object could go down her windpipe.)

2) If the object is in the ear and you can't see it, CALL A DOCTOR.

STOMACHACHE

Sometimes a tummy ache just means that the child has to go to the bathroom. Sometimes it means she's getting the flu. The excitement of a new sitter or the stress of saying good-bye to her mom and dad can also bring on a stomach pain. Here are a few ways to try to take away the pain:

1) Have the child lie on her back and gently rub her tummy.

2) Often a warm bath will take away the pain.

3) If it seems like just a nervous stomach, a small glass of carbonated drink such as 7UP or Coke will help settle her down.

4) If the stomachache seems severe and continues for more than an hour—CALL THE PARENTS.

TOOTH INJURY

The child is running, he falls down, hits his head on the coffee table, and knocks a tooth out. What do you do?

1) First, deal with the child's pain. Sit him in a chair and try to remain calm. Wet a washcloth with cool water and have him press it to the place where the tooth either broke off or fell out.

2) If the whole tooth was knocked out, there is the possibility that it was a baby tooth and ready to fall out. However, CALL THE PARENTS and they can call the dentist. The dentist may be able to put the tooth back, so speed is important.

3) If the tooth is knocked out completely, pick it up and wrap it gently in a cloth, or put the tooth in a jar or glass of water until the parents get home. Don't try to wipe it off.

VOMITING

Vomiting can be brought on by the flu or something the child ate that didn't agree with her or just plain excitability. Vomit can be pretty disgusting, but try not to let the child know how you feel about it. It's very frightening to a child and the most important thing you can do is remain calm. Try and act as if it's just "a bad burp" and let her know it will be over in a minute.

1) If the child is lying down when she starts vomiting, help her sit up. Don't worry about where the vomit is going. (Grab a towel, a pan, or a pillowcase if one is handy.)

2) Calmly help her into the bathroom and wipe off any vomit that may be on her clothes.

3) If the vomiting seems to have stopped and she wants to go back to bed or lie down, place a towel and a pan or a bowl next to the bed, just in case. She may want you to place a cool washcloth on her forehead.

4) She may be thirsty because vomiting dehydrates the body. Let her have little sips of water (not milk) or Coke with the fizz stirred out of it. Fill a glass with Coke and spin a fork around in it until it's very frothy. Wait for thirty minutes, then give her about a tablespoon every fifteen minutes.

5) Wait for at least an hour before giving her any food. It could start the process all over again. If she wants something to eat, try a saltine cracker.

If the child seems to be getting worse, with fever, chills, and stomach pain, call the parents.

If a baby spits up, don't panic—it's perfectly normal. Especially after eating. Sometimes you may see projectile vomiting immediately after drinking a bottle. (That's when it shoots across the room. Ew ick!) You only need to worry if that happens continuously. If it's very violent or the baby is inconsolable—CALL THE PARENTS.

NOTE: If the child has fallen and is unconscious and vomiting— don't move him. Clear his throat of the vomit and then CALL 911 (OR AN AMBULANCE.)

PART V
MY
BABY-SITTING
RECORD BOOK

MY CLIENT DIRECTORY
■

I always check the BSC's client directory
before going to a baby-sitting job. Besides
reminding me of any special instructions for
that family, it helps me decide what to bring
in my Kid-Kit.
                                    —Claudia

MY CLIENT DIRECTORY

■

FAMILY'S NAME: _____

ADDRESS: _____ PHONE: _____

CHILDREN'S NAMES: AGE:

_____

_____

_____

FAVORITE TOY: _____

FAVORITE BOOK: _____

FAVORITE FOOD: _____

SPECIAL INSTRUCTIONS (Allergies, medications, etc.):

_____

_____

_____

_____

_____

EMERGENCY NUMBERS:

_____

_____

_____

THEIR DOCTOR: _____

MY CLIENT DIRECTORY

■

FAMILY'S NAME: _____

ADDRESS: _____ PHONE: _____

CHILDREN'S NAMES: AGE:

_____

_____

_____

FAVORITE TOY: _____

FAVORITE BOOK: _____

FAVORITE FOOD: _____

SPECIAL INSTRUCTIONS (Allergies, medications, etc.):

_____

_____

_____

_____

_____

EMERGENCY NUMBERS:

_____

_____

_____

THEIR DOCTOR: _____

MY CLIENT DIRECTORY

■

FAMILY'S NAME: _____

ADDRESS: _____ PHONE: _____

CHILDREN'S NAMES: AGE:

_____

_____

_____

FAVORITE TOY: _____

FAVORITE BOOK: _____

FAVORITE FOOD: _____

SPECIAL INSTRUCTIONS (Allergies, medications, etc.):

_____

_____

_____

_____

_____

EMERGENCY NUMBERS:

_____

_____

_____

THEIR DOCTOR: _____

MY CLIENT DIRECTORY

■

FAMILY'S NAME: _____

ADDRESS: _____ PHONE: _____

CHILDREN'S NAMES: _____ AGE:

_____

_____

_____

FAVORITE TOY: _____

FAVORITE BOOK: _____

FAVORITE FOOD: _____

SPECIAL INSTRUCTIONS (Allergies, medications, etc.):

_____

_____

_____

_____

_____

EMERGENCY NUMBERS:

_____

_____

_____

THEIR DOCTOR: _____

MY CLIENT DIRECTORY

■

FAMILY'S NAME: _____

ADDRESS: _____ PHONE: _____

CHILDREN'S NAMES: AGE:

_____

_____

_____

FAVORITE TOY: _____

FAVORITE BOOK: _____

FAVORITE FOOD: _____

SPECIAL INSTRUCTIONS (Allergies, medications, etc.):

_____

_____

_____

_____

_____

EMERGENCY NUMBERS:

_____

_____

_____

THEIR DOCTOR: _____

MY CLIENT DIRECTORY

■

FAMILY'S NAME: _____

ADDRESS: _____ PHONE: _____

CHILDREN'S NAMES: AGE:

_____

_____

_____

FAVORITE TOY: _____

FAVORITE BOOK: _____

FAVORITE FOOD: _____

SPECIAL INSTRUCTIONS (Allergies, medications, etc.):

_____

_____

_____

_____

EMERGENCY NUMBERS:

_____

_____

_____

THEIR DOCTOR: _____

MY CLIENT DIRECTORY
■

FAMILY'S NAME: _____

ADDRESS: _____ PHONE: _____

CHILDREN'S NAMES: AGE:

_____

_____

_____

FAVORITE TOY: _____

FAVORITE BOOK: _____

FAVORITE FOOD: _____

SPECIAL INSTRUCTIONS (Allergies, medications, etc.):

_____

_____

_____

_____

EMERGENCY NUMBERS:

_____

_____

_____

THEIR DOCTOR: _____

MY BABY-SITTING SCHEDULE
■

In the record book I
use a calendar to keep
track of our weekly
schedules — such as Jessi's
ballet lessons and Kristy's
Krushers' practices. I also
write down the name of
the client and date and
time of each of our
baby-sitting jobs.
— Mary Anne

MONTH: _____

WEEK 1:	MON	TUE	WED	THUR	FRI	SAT	SUN
WEEK 2:	MON	TUE	WED	THUR	FRI	SAT	SUN
WEEK 3:	MON	TUE	WED	THUR	FRI	SAT	SUN
WEEK 4:	MON	TUE	WED	THUR	FRI	SAT	SUN
WEEK 5:	MON	TUE	WED	THUR	FRI	SAT	SUN

MONTH: _____

WEEK 1:	MON	TUE	WED	THUR	FRI	SAT	SUN
WEEK 2:	MON	TUE	WED	THUR	FRI	SAT	SUN
WEEK 3:	MON	TUE	WED	THUR	FRI	SAT	SUN
WEEK 4:	MON	TUE	WED	THUR	FRI	SAT	SUN
WEEK 5:	MON	TUE	WED	THUR	FRI	SAT	SUN

MONTH: _____

WEEK 1:	MON	TUE	WED	THUR	FRI	SAT	SUN
WEEK 2:	MON	TUE	WED	THUR	FRI	SAT	SUN
WEEK 3:	MON	TUE	WED	THUR	FRI	SAT	SUN
WEEK 4:	MON	TUE	WED	THUR	FRI	SAT	SUN
WEEK 5:	MON	TUE	WED	THUR	FRI	SAT	SUN

MONTH: _____

WEEK 1:	MON	TUE	WED	THUR	FRI	SAT	SUN
WEEK 2:	MON	TUE	WED	THUR	FRI	SAT	SUN
WEEK 3:	MON	TUE	WED	THUR	FRI	SAT	SUN
WEEK 4:	MON	TUE	WED	THUR	FRI	SAT	SUN
WEEK 5:	MON	TUE	WED	THUR	FRI	SAT	SUN

MONTH: _____

WEEK 1:	MON	TUE	WED	THUR	FRI	SAT	SUN
WEEK 2:	MON	TUE	WED	THUR	FRI	SAT	SUN
WEEK 3:	MON	TUE	WED	THUR	FRI	SAT	SUN
WEEK 4:	MON	TUE	WED	THUR	FRI	SAT	SUN
WEEK 5:	MON	TUE	WED	THUR	FRI	SAT	SUN

MONTH: _____

WEEK 1:	MON	TUE	WED	THUR	FRI	SAT	SUN
WEEK 2:	MON	TUE	WED	THUR	FRI	SAT	SUN
WEEK 3:	MON	TUE	WED	THUR	FRI	SAT	SUN
WEEK 4:	MON	TUE	WED	THUR	FRI	SAT	SUN
WEEK 5:	MON	TUE	WED	THUR	FRI	SAT	SUN

MONTH: _____

WEEK 1:	MON	TUE	WED	THUR	FRI	SAT	SUN
WEEK 2:	MON	TUE	WED	THUR	FRI	SAT	SUN
WEEK 3:	MON	TUE	WED	THUR	FRI	SAT	SUN
WEEK 4:	MON	TUE	WED	THUR	FRI	SAT	SUN
WEEK 5:	MON	TUE	WED	THUR	FRI	SAT	SUN

MONTH: _____

WEEK 1:	MON	TUE	WED	THUR	FRI	SAT	SUN
WEEK 2:	MON	TUE	WED	THUR	FRI	SAT	SUN
WEEK 3:	MON	TUE	WED	THUR	FRI	SAT	SUN
WEEK 4:	MON	TUE	WED	THUR	FRI	SAT	SUN
WEEK 5:	MON	TUE	WED	THUR	FRI	SAT	SUN

MONTH: _____

WEEK 1:	MON	TUE	WED	THUR	FRI	SAT	SUN
WEEK 2:	MON	TUE	WED	THUR	FRI	SAT	SUN
WEEK 3:	MON	TUE	WED	THUR	FRI	SAT	SUN
WEEK 4:	MON	TUE	WED	THUR	FRI	SAT	SUN
WEEK 5:	MON	TUE	WED	THUR	FRI	SAT	SUN

MONTH: _____

WEEK 1:	MON	TUE	WED	THUR	FRI	SAT	SUN
WEEK 2:	MON	TUE	WED	THUR	FRI	SAT	SUN
WEEK 3:	MON	TUE	WED	THUR	FRI	SAT	SUN
WEEK 4:	MON	TUE	WED	THUR	FRI	SAT	SUN
WEEK 5:	MON	TUE	WED	THUR	FRI	SAT	SUN

MONTH: _____

WEEK 1:	MON	TUE	WED	THUR	FRI	SAT	SUN
WEEK 2:	MON	TUE	WED	THUR	FRI	SAT	SUN
WEEK 3:	MON	TUE	WED	THUR	FRI	SAT	SUN
WEEK 4:	MON	TUE	WED	THUR	FRI	SAT	SUN
WEEK 5:	MON	TUE	WED	THUR	FRI	SAT	SUN

MONTH: _____

WEEK 1:	MON	TUE	WED	THUR	FRI	SAT	SUN
WEEK 2:	MON	TUE	WED	THUR	FRI	SAT	SUN
WEEK 3:	MON	TUE	WED	THUR	FRI	SAT	SUN
WEEK 4:	MON	TUE	WED	THUR	FRI	SAT	SUN
WEEK 5:	MON	TUE	WED	THUR	FRI	SAT	SUN

MONTH: _____

WEEK 1:	MON	TUE	WED	THUR	FRI	SAT	SUN
WEEK 2:	MON	TUE	WED	THUR	FRI	SAT	SUN
WEEK 3:	MON	TUE	WED	THUR	FRI	SAT	SUN
WEEK 4:	MON	TUE	WED	THUR	FRI	SAT	SUN
WEEK 5:	MON	TUE	WED	THUR	FRI	SAT	SUN

MONTH: _____

WEEK 1:	MON	TUE	WED	THUR	FRI	SAT	SUN
WEEK 2:	MON	TUE	WED	THUR	FRI	SAT	SUN
WEEK 3:	MON	TUE	WED	THUR	FRI	SAT	SUN
WEEK 4:	MON	TUE	WED	THUR	FRI	SAT	SUN
WEEK 5:	MON	TUE	WED	THUR	FRI	SAT	SUN

MY BABY-SITTING EARNINGS
■

Keeping a record of your earnings helps
you budget money for your Kid-Kit,
money for savings and, best of all,
money for fun.

— Stacey

Date	Rate per Hour	Hours Worked	Total Earned

Date	Rate per Hour	Hours Worked	Total Earned

Date	Rate per Hour	Hours Worked	Total Earned

Date	Rate per Hour	Hours Worked	Total Earned

MY BABY-SITTING NOTEBOOK

■

The notebook is like a journal. We use it to record our experiences on the job and any special thoughts we have about our clients and their kids.

—Kristy

THE BABY-SITTERS CLUB®

by Ann M. Martin

More titles... ▶

❑ MG44970-2	#49 Claudia and the Genius of Elm Street	$3.25
❑ MG44969-9	#50 Dawn's Big Date	$3.25
❑ MG44968-0	#51 Stacey's Ex-Best Friend	$3.25
❑ MG44966-4	#52 Mary Anne + 2 Many Babies	$3.25
❑ MG44967-2	#53 Kristy for President	$3.25
❑ MG44965-6	#54 Mallory and the Dream Horse	$3.25
❑ MG44964-8	#55 Jessi's Gold Medal	$3.25
❑ MG45657-1	#56 Keep Out, Claudia!	$3.25
❑ MG45658-X	#57 Dawn Saves the Planet	$3.25
❑ MG45659-8	#58 Stacey's Choice	$3.25
❑ MG45660-1	#59 Mallory Hates Boys (and Gym)	$3.25
❑ MG45662-8	#60 Mary Anne's Makeover	$3.50
❑ MG45663-6	#61 Jessi's and the Awful Secret	$3.50
❑ MG45664-4	#62 Kristy and the Worst Kid Ever	$3.50
❑ MG45665-2	#63 Claudia's ~~Freind~~ Friend	$3.50
❑ MG45666-0	#64 Dawn's Family Feud	$3.50
❑ MG45667-9	#65 Stacey's Big Crush	$3.50
❑ MG45575-3	Logan's Story Special Edition Readers' Request	$3.25
❑ MG44240-6	Baby-sitters on Board! Super Special #1	$3.95
❑ MG44239-2	Baby-sitters' Summer Vacation Super Special #2	$3.95
❑ MG43973-1	Baby-sitters' Winter Vacation Super Special #3	$3.95
❑ MG42493-9	Baby-sitters' Island Adventure Super Special #4	$3.95
❑ MG43575-2	California Girls! Super Special #5	$3.95
❑ MG43576-0	New York, New York! Super Special #6	$3.95
❑ MG44963-X	Snowbound Super Special #7	$3.95
❑ MG44962-X	Baby-sitters at Shadow Lake Super Special #8	$3.95
❑ MG45661-X	Starring the Baby-sitters Club Super Special #9	$3.95

Available wherever you buy books...or use this order form.

Scholastic Inc., P.O. Box 7502, 2931 E. McCarty Street, Jefferson City, MO 65102

Please send me the books I have checked above. I am enclosing $———
(please add $2.00 to cover shipping and handling). Send check or money order - no
cash or C.O.D.s please.

Name ——————————————————————————————————

Address ——————————————————————————————————

City———————————————— State/Zip ————————————————
Please allow four to six weeks for delivery. Offer good in the U.S. only. Sorry, mail orders are not
available to residents of Canada. Prices subject to change.

BSC1292

Join the new online Baby-sitters Club on the PRODIGY® service.

★PRODIGY. Service®

TALK TO ANN M. MARTIN IN A WEEKLY COLUMN

READ ALL NEW STORIES STARRING THE BSC GANG

VOTE ON STORY ENDINGS

MAKE FRIENDS ALL ACROSS THE COUNTRY

TAKE POLLS AND PLAY TRIVIA GAMES

For more information, have your parents call

1-800-776-0838 ext.261